CRAPS STRATEGY

CRAPS STRATEGY

How to Play to Win at Casino Craps

Michael Benson

The Lyons Press
Guilford, Connecticut
An imprint of The Globe Pequot Press

The Lyons Press is an imprint of The Globe Pequot Press.

10 9 8 7 6 5 4 3 2

Printed in Canada

ISBN 1-59228-298-9

The Library of Congress has cataloged an earlier edition as follows:

Benson, Michael.
   Craps strategy : how to play to win at casino craps /
   Michael Benson ; [Illustrations by Jim A. Pearson].
      p. cm.
   Includes bibliographical references.
   ISBN 1-58574-347-X
   1. Craps (Game) 2. Dice games.
I. Title.

GV1303.B46 2001
795.1'2—dc21   2001038588
                                                CIP

For Mark, Tim, and David Thomas Treu:
May their luck always run hot

ACKNOWLEDGMENTS

The author wishes to thank the following persons: Rita Benson, Keith Brenner, Jake Elwell; Enrica Gadler; Tony & Marie Grasso; Eric Ketchum; Paul McCaffrey; Greig O'Brien; Bert Randolph Sugar.

CONTENTS

INTRODUCTION
THE JOY OF CRAPS: WHEN YOU'RE HOT, YOU'RE HOT

Craps is not just the oldest game being played in today's casinos, but it is the most exciting as well. The bells and whistles may be coming from the slot machines, but that whooping and hollering of joy you hear is coming from the craps tables.

You've heard the expression, "When you're hot, you're hot." Nowhere is that more true than at the craps table. Dice, when they get hot, have been known to practically set the casino on fire.

Catch a hot streak by the tail and you can roll your way to millions in five incredible minutes of action. (Ah, but that's the trick. There is another half to the axiom which states, "When you're not, you're not." Dice can cool off faster than a gold digger who has just discovered you are broke.)

1

With casinos changing the rules of blackjack to thwart the skill of card-counters, craps is quickly becoming the "fairest" game in the casino.

Played smartly, you can reduce the house advantage to near zero. Using the money management and betting progression techniques explained here, you can absolutely maximize your chances of winning at the craps table.

DETERMINE YOUR OWN FATE

More than any other game in the casino, craps is fun to play. Sure, it is exciting to watch the roulette wheel go round, wondering which driveway the silver ball is going to park in—but you don't get to spin the wheel yourself.

No matter how long you play blackjack in a casino, it is never your turn to deal. But when you play craps, wait your turn and you'll get a chance to roll the dice—to determine your own fate, if you will—not to mention the fate of everyone else playing at the table.

With the exception of blackjack, all casino games have fixed percentages against the player. That is the house advantage, which is why the owners can pump zillions of dollars into their boardwalk casinos, whereas those who spend too much time playing in those casinos often are forced to sleep under the boardwalk.

Each spin of the roulette wheel makes money for the casino. Most people believe that the same is true of each roll of the dice at the craps table, and that everyone who plays craps for hours on end will end up, eventually, giving all of their money to the casino.

Well, I am here to tell you it ain't necessarily so.

PLAY SMART AND WIN

Although it is impossible for the player to have an advantage over the house when playing craps—after all, the casinos determine the rules of the game and how much they pay out for each winning bet—it is possible, by playing smart craps, to reduce the house advantage to something less than half of one percent.

This is why it is frequently possible to win at the craps table. Especially if you have the knack of betting a lot when you are hot and a little when you are cold.

Casinos, much to the delight of smart folks, make much of their money from bad (i.e. stupid) gamblers. Next time you are at a craps table, check out those who are betting the "Hardway" bets.

Or those that place Field bets.

Or bets on Any Craps, Any Seven, and Any Eleven. It has been said that a fool and his money are soon parted, and nowhere is that more true than at the craps table.

(Don't worry if you don't know what some of these terms mean. This book contains a complete introductory course in how to play craps. All will be made clear soon enough.)

It has also been said that the difference between the real odds and the odds that the casino pays off for these bets when they win is so large that they should fall under the anti-usury laws.

The house advantage against those "Hardway" players are sometimes larger than 20 percent. Those who place number bets are doing a little better but not much. These craps players would be better served by putting a big "L" on the middle of their foreheads and simply handing their shirts to the dealers.

FAST ACTION

Craps is fascinating to many casino-hounds because the action is so fast—money is won and lost with every roll of the dice—and there is such a wide variety of possible plays. And, within those plays is a wide range of odds. Thus one player can be making money while another player is losing his shirt, even though they are standing beside one another at the same craps table.

For the same reason, craps is big on tall tales. Everyone has a story and practically none of them are true. With the possible exception of fishing, craps begets more whoppers than any other activity, so beware of wagering based on a "system" explained to you in a bar.

And beware of hype. Not only do the casinos use it to get you through their doors, but so do the gambling experts promising can't-lose systems that are sure to make you a millionaire.

They can't. You won't. But that doesn't mean that there aren't some extremely useful craps strategies out there. This book is made up of them.

So come with me now to a joyous place, to the land where bones don't rattle, they roll; where Fate bounces this way and that, spinning seemingly forever on a corner before falling into place, determining the winners from the losers; where Papa is perpetually in need of a new pair of shoes.

A NOTE ON STYLE

In this book, a number that appears on a die or dice, will be capitalized. For example, "I rolled a Three four times."

CHAPTER ONE
GETTING ORIENTED: THE TABLE

The craps table is usually about three and a half feet wide and twelve feet long. Covered in felt, most often green, it is marked with blocks on which players place their chips.

Which block you place your chips on determines the type of bet you are making. The design on the table is known as the *layout*. If, at any time, you are uncertain about where to place your chips to place a certain kind of bet, be sure to ask your dealer (you'll find out who he is in a second) and he (or she) will be glad to help you.

The blocks on one half of the table are repeated in identical order on the other half, so players on either side can place their bets with equal ease. The table is wooden and the edges are padded so players can lean on it comfortably. There is a trough around the edge of the table in which players can keep their chips.

7

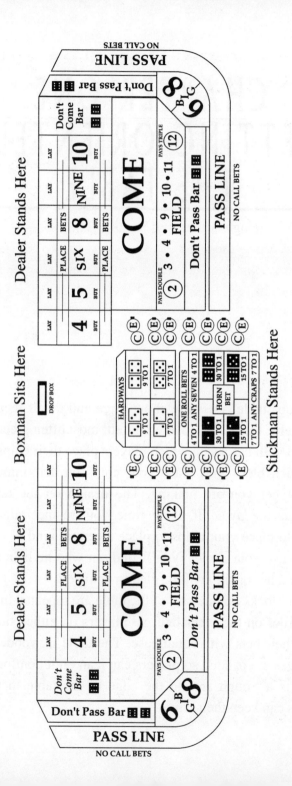

DON'T SQUEEZE IN

The players' section of the table is divided into twenty-two sections, to keep to a minimum confusion over whose chips are whose. However, because the individual sections for players are so slender—while players often are not—only fifteen or so players can play at a table at once without things becoming uncomfortably cramped.

If a table is crowded, do not try to push your way in. There is no quicker way to create bad vibes than to take a crowded situation and make it worse. I have seen fights start over this very point.

If a table appears full, it is. Find someplace else.

TAKE TURNS

Players take turns shooting the dice. You do not have to shoot the dice if you do not want to. You can simply pass the dice along and skip your turn. If you do choose to roll dem bones, try to bounce them off the table's inner wall. This visibly demonstrates that you are not cheating.

Most casinos have all of their craps tables in the same section, most often arranged in circles of eight tables each. These circles are known as pits.

WHOSE CHIPS ARE WHOSE?

When the dealer puts your winnings on the table he will put those chips in the same box in which the bet was placed, but will place the chips in the section of that box that corresponds to your position at the table.

When placing your bets, you should also place your chips in the portion of the box that corresponds to your position at the table. This will make it easier for the dealer to determine whose bet is whose and help assure that you will be given all of the winnings you deserve (without an argument).

THE CREW

THE BOXMAN

On one side of the table is an indentation. Three of the casino employees who run the table are on this side. The person in the center is known as the boxman. The boxman keeps his eyes on the other casino employees working at the table to make sure that everything is going smoothly and according to the rules. If necessary the boxman is called upon to settle disputes, so he tries to keep his eyes on everything at once.

THE DEALERS

The dealers stand on either side of the boxman, so that every player has a dealer nearby. Think of it as a bar with a bartender at either end. The dealers collect the losing bets and pay off the winning ones. They are there to be helpful so if you have any question, the dealer in front of you is the person to ask.

Remember, they are human and make mistakes. Many dealers are bored but few are evil. Keep your eyes on your chips to make sure that the dealer does not pay off your neighbor for your bet, or pay off your bet in the wrong amount.

THE STICKMAN

Opposite the boxman, stands another employee known as the stickman. The stickman uses a long, L-shaped stick, to move the dice.

It is also the stickman's responsibility to call out the number once the dice come to a stop. A good stickman will also keep a running commentary going so that the players may more easily follow the ramifications of each result.

The stickman stands at the center of the table. He handles the bets that are placed in the center section. (We will get to which those are later.) He also makes sure that all bets are in place before he returns the dice to the shooter.

The dealers and the stickman stand while the boxman sits. Each table has a four-man crew—although the boxman is not technically known as part of the crew—with one of the four always on a twenty-minute break. That way, the theory goes, the employees stay refreshed while the action at the table never stops.

THE FLOORMAN

In addition to the employees who actually work around the table, there is also a floorman, who is usually assigned to several tables at once.

The floorman makes sure that the players all have drinks and are comfortable. If a player has credit with the casino, the floorman keeps track of the credit and gives the dealers permission to honor that credit with chips. If a dispute cannot be handled by a table's boxman, then the floorman might be consulted.

The floorman, in turn, reports to the pit boss, who is the casino employee in charge of the entire pit. And the entire operation is watched by omnipresent surveillance cameras—the infamous "Eye in the Sky"—mounted here, there, and everywhere.

HOW TO CONVERT YOUR CASH

When you first get to the craps table, you give your cash to the dealer nearest you and he gives you the appropriate number of chips in return. You play only in chips. For legal reasons, the dealers are not allowed to take cash from your hand and you are not allowed to take chips from theirs.

You must place your money on the box on the table marked "COME." The dealer will then take the money, place the chips in the "COME" box and then you can take your chips. If you already have chips you may just walk up and place a bet. The dealer will figure it out.

"CASH PLAYS"

If you have cash only and want to bet on the roll of the dice that is about to take place then and there, you can place cash on the layout and say, "Cash plays."

If your bet wins, you are paid off in chips. If you lose, you still need chips because your cash is gone.

CHIPS ARE REAL MONEY

I know I shouldn't have to tell you this, but chips are real money, not *play money*. Some people have the same problem when playing with chips as they do when spending foreign currency. Sound familiar?

They can't quite come to grips with the fact that this stuff is every bit as precious as the dead presidents they are used to carrying in their wallet.

They end up spending the stuff—chips, foreign currency—as if it were Monopoly money. They take risks that they wouldn't take in a million years if they were playing with *E Pluribus Unum* legal tender.

KNOW THE TABLE MINIMUM

Be sure you know the "table minimum" before you start to play. Many tables have a $10 or $25 minimum, and if this is richer than your blood, you shouldn't be there.

In most casinos, $5 is the lowest minimum you will find at a craps table, although there are places in Las Vegas—where the competition is toughest between casinos—where you can find a table with a $1 minimum.

YOUR TURN TO ROLL

When it is your turn to shoot the dice, the first thing you must do is make a "Come Out" roll. If you roll a Seven or Eleven, your dice have "passed." Certain bets will win or lose and you get to roll again.

If you roll a Two, Three, or Twelve—these are known as "craps." Again, certain bets will win or lose and you get to roll again. (You cannot "crap out" in a modern casino craps game. That is, you cannot lose your turn by rolling craps. You retain your turn to shoot the dice even if you roll craps on the come out roll.)

If you roll any other number (Four, Five, Six, Eight, Nine, or Ten), then this number becomes your "point." To help the players follow the action, the dealer will then take a small disc, called the "marker puck"—with "on" written on one side and "off" on the other-and place it, "on" side up, in the box on the table marked with the number that is now your point.

The object then, for you, is to roll the number that is your point again before you roll a Seven. This is also known as a "pass." (Most of the betting in craps has to do with whether or not the shooter will roll his point before he rolls a Seven.)

If you succeed you start over with another come out roll. If not, if you roll a Seven *before* you roll your point, then the next person gets to shoot the dice.

THE DICE

The dice used for craps are six-sided cubes with one to six dots on each side, always arranged so that the dots on opposite sides add up to seven.

The dice used in casinos are usually made of clear red plastic and bear identification markings so that it is impossible for someone to substitute loaded dice.

When you roll a pair of dice—one of the cubes is a die, a pair of them is dice—there are thirty-six possible combinations that can come up.

Any number from Two (One and One) to Twelve (Six and Six) can come up. The odds that you will roll a Two or a Twelve—as we have seen—are therefore 35–1, since there is only one way they can come up so over the long run they will appear once for every thirty-six rolls of the dice.

The chart below shows the various number combinations that result from two dice. The more frequently a number appears on the chart, the greater its probability of being rolled.

Die A

	1	2	3	4	5	6
1	2	3	4	5	6	7
2	3	4	5	6	7	8
3	4	5	6	7	8	9
4	5	6	7	8	9	10
5	6	7	8	9	10	11
6	7	8	9	10	11	12

(Die B labels the rows)

HOUSE ADVANTAGE

Before we learn the different types of bets available at the craps table, let's get used to one universal truth: For every bet the house has a certain advantage over you.

That is, the chances that what you are betting on is actually going to happen are always greater than the casino's payoff would reflect.

For example, if you bet that the next roll of the dice will be a Twelve, the odds are 35–1 (read this "35 to 1") that this will occur. That means that, for every thirty-six times the dice are rolled, the chances are that only one roll will be a Twelve.

The problem is that the casino will pay off at only 30–1 when that Twelve comes up, so over the long run, they make almost fourteen cents on every dollar that is bet on the Twelve.

Now don't panic. The house advantage, sometimes called the vig, is not always that high, and determining which types of bets offer the most fair payoffs is a big part of learning how to maximize your chances of winning at the craps table.

How did I figure out the odds of rolling a Twelve? Let me explain.

DOING THE MATH

As I said, the reason that most people lose at craps in a casino is that the house has made up the rules in their favor. The game is rigged.

For example, if you bet $5 that, on the next roll of the dice, "Snake Eyes" (One, One) will appear, you are being played for a sucker. Play that bet for every roll of the dice for an extended period of time and eventually all of the money which once upon a time had been yours will be the casino's.

Even if Snake Eyes comes up once for every thirty-six rolls of the dice, as would be expected, you will steadily lose your money because you will win only $150 each time it happens, rather than the $175 you would have to make to break even.

COUNTING THE COMBINATIONS

There are only two ways to roll a Three and an Eleven. A Three can be rolled with a Two and a One, as well as with a One and a Two. An Eleven can be rolled with a Six and a Five, as well as with a Five and a Six. So the odds of rolling a Three and the odds of rolling an Eleven on any single roll are always 17½ to 1.

There are three ways to roll a Four and three ways to roll a Ten. A Four can be rolled with

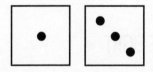

A One and a Three . . .

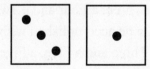

A Three and a One . . .

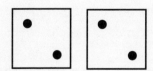

And a Two and a Two.

THE TEN

A Ten can be rolled with a Four and a Six, a Six and a Four, and two Fives. So the odds of rolling a Four, and the odds of rolling a Ten are always 11–1 on any single roll of the dice.

THE FIVE AND THE NINE

There are four ways apiece to roll a Five and a Nine. The Five can be rolled with a One and a Four, a Four and a One, a Two and a Three, and a Three and a Two.

The Nine can be rolled with a Six and a Three, a Three and a Six, a Five and a Four, and a Four and a Five. So the odds of rolling a Five, and the odds of rolling a Nine are both 8–1 on any roll of the dice.

THE SIX AND THE EIGHT

A Six and an Eight can each be rolled in five different ways. The Six can be made with a One and a Five, a Five and a One, a Three and a Three, a Four and a Two, and a Two and a Four. An Eight can be accomplished with a Two and a Six, a Six and a Two, a Three and a Five, a Five and a Three, and a Four and a Four. So the odds of rolling an Eight and the odds of rolling a Six, are both 6.2–1.

LUCKY SEVEN

The easiest number to roll is a Seven. There are six different ways to do it: a One and a Six, a Six and a One, a Two and a Five, a Five and a Two, a Three and a Four, and a

Four and a Three. The odds of rolling a Seven on any single roll are 5–1.

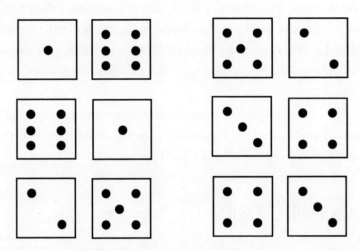

Total	Number of combinations	Probability	0dds
Two	one	2.78 percent	35–1
Three	two	5.56 percent	17–1
Four	three	8.33 percent	11–1
Five	four	11.11 percent	8–1
Six	five	13.89 percent	6.2–1
Seven	six	16.67 percent	5–1
Eight	five	13.89 percent	6.2–1
Nine	four	11.11 percent	8–1
Ten	three	8.33 percent	11–1
Eleven	two	5.56 percent	17–1
Twelve	one	2.78 percent	35–1

NO CHEATING

For starters, this is not a book about so-called "dice control." I am not going to teach you where to put your thumb on a die and how to hold your shoulders when you throw the dice so that you increase the number of Sevens you throw.

If it works, it's cheating—and even though it might work for a few sleight-of-hand experts, it won't work for you. You'll get caught and you'll get tossed.

RAISE YOUR CRAPS IQ

This book, instead, is going to teach you how to maximize your chances of winning at the craps table by playing smart.

If you are looking for a quiet game, craps is not for you. Like baseball infielders and boxing trainers, craps players "chatter" while playing, keeping a running monologue of axioms, postulations, and queries of the Almighty— expressing one's need for a new pair of shoes is a common utterance—meant to encourage positive karma.

THE RULES

The rules of craps are actually very easy. If you are rolling the dice, you can win in a couple of ways:

- You can roll a Seven or an Eleven on your first roll.
- Or, if you roll a Four, Five, Six, Eight, Nine, Ten, or Eleven, it is called your Come Point and, if you roll that number again before rolling a Seven, you win.

- A roller loses, and must pass the dice, if he or she rolls a Seven before rolling the Come Point.
- A roller loses but gets to shoot again, if he or she rolls a Two (Snake Eyes), Three, or Twelve (Box Cars) on the first roll.

Those are the basics of the game, but only a small part of the story.

TAKE A RIDE ON THE PASS LINE

At a craps table, the action is hardly limited to the person with the dice. Everyone else gets to play too, betting on whether or not the roller will succeed.

The most common bet at a craps table is the Pass Line bet. This bet is always placed before a new shooter starts to roll, after a shooter has made his point and is seeking to establish a new point, or after the shooter has a natural (a Seven or an Eleven on the first roll) or a craps (a Two, Three, or Twelve on the first roll).

Ah, but that's a subject for our next chapter, which will teach you about the many types of bets you can make at a craps table.

BEWARE OF ODDS TERMINOLOGY

When odds are said to be five-for-one, this means that, if you bet $1 and win, you get $5 back. You won $4, plus you get the $1 that you bet back. This is most commonly called 4–1 (read four-to-one). So, if you see a "for" between the odds numbers rather than a "to," that probably means that the casino is trying to make their payoffs seem better than they really are.

CHAPTER TWO
TYPES OF BETS

There are many different types of bets you can make when playing craps. Some are a lot more intelligent than others. Once again, I'll start with the most popular.

PASS LINE

You place your chips in the box marked Pass Line or Win Line in order to bet that the shooter will win. The Pass Line is sometimes called the "front line." The Pass Line bet must be made before the shooter has established his point—that is, either on the shooter's first roll, after he shoots a natural, or after he has made a point and is seeking to establish a new point.

If the shooter rolls a Seven or an Eleven on the first roll, you win even money. (Ten dollars back on a five-dollar bet.)

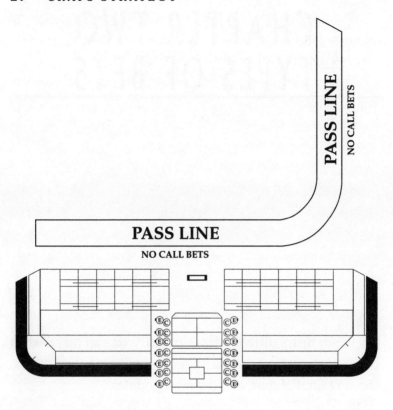

If the shooter rolls craps (Two, Three, or Twelve) on the first roll, you lose. (As mentioned, rolling craps on a Come Out roll does not complete the shooter's turn—sometimes called the "shooter's hand"—and he or she gets to roll again.)

If the shooter rolls any other number, it becomes his "point." And the shooter must now try to make the point, before he rolls another Seven.

If the shooter rolls his or her point again before rolling a Seven, you win. A roll of Seven, after the point is established, completes the shooter's turn and you lose. The dice then move to a new shooter.

Once the shooter has established his point, only the point number and a Seven are of consequence—at least to those who are betting on the Pass Line.

If, for example, the shooter rolls a Four on his Come Out roll, he could roll, say, a Two, a Twelve, a Five, and a Six on his next four rolls of the dice and they don't mean anything—except to those who are betting on the results of each individual roll of the dice, but we'll get to that.

To the player who is betting on the Pass Line, those results are meaningless. The bet is now that a Four will come up before a Seven. If the Four comes up first, you win. If the Seven comes up, you lose.

To review, if you bet two chips on the Pass Line, a Come Out roll of Seven or Eleven wins you even money. A Come Out roll of Two, Three, or Twelve (craps) loses.

A Come Out roll of Four, Five, Six, Eight, Nine, or Ten becomes the point and after that, you win if the point number is repeated before a Seven is rolled. You lose if the Seven is rolled before the point.

This is the most popular bet at the table. At any given moment most craps players will have chips on the Pass Line. Because most players are rooting for the shooter to make his passes, craps players tend to feel like teammates at the table, with everyone rooting for the same outcomes.

There are two reasons that the Pass Line is craps' most popular bet: 1) you are betting with the shooter, thus creating good karma at the table; and 2) the house advantage is only 1.41 percent. That is, for every hundred dollars you bet on the Pass Line, over the long run you should expect to lose only $1.41.

DON'T PASS

To bet that the shooter will lose, place your bet before the shooter's Come Out roll on the area of the table labeled "Don't Pass." This area is called the Don't Pass Line and sometimes the Back Line.

Like the Pass Line bet, this bet must be made before the shooter's Come Out (first) roll. (To help the players follow the action, the dealers will always announce the Come Out roll by saying something to the effect of: "Dice coming out!") If the shooter rolls a Three or a Twelve on the first roll you win.

If the shooter rolls a Seven or an Eleven on the first roll, you lose.

The rules concerning rolling a Two on the Come Out roll vary depending on the casino. In some places a Two on the Come Out roll wins even money for the Don't Pass bettor.

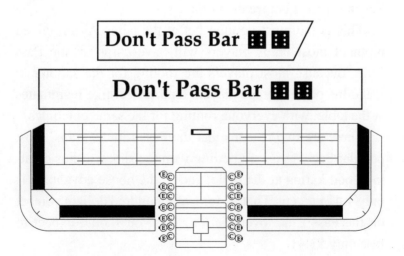

In other places—cheaper places, to be blunt—if the shooter rolls a Two, it is a stand off (a push), and no one wins. No money exchanges hands.

If the shooter rolls any other number, it becomes his or her point. A Seven must be thrown before this point is rolled again in order for you to win.

If the point is rolled before a Seven, you lose. Don't Pass bets may be removed at any time by asking the dealer to take them down.

The house advantage for Don't Pass bets is just a tad smaller than that for the Pass Line. The vig for the Don't Bettors is 1.40 percent, so you should expect to lose $1.40 for every hundred dollars you place on the Don't Pass box.

Be aware that "Don't Bettors" are not the most popular folks in the casino. They are thought to bring long spells of doom to a table. That's because most players bet with the shooter, so a Don't Bettor is, in essence, betting that everyone else will lose.

COME BET

The Come bet is very similar to the Pass Line bet. However, with the come bet, the bet must be placed only after the shooter has established a point.

After that the bet behaves just like a Pass Line bet.

If, on the first roll of the dice after the Come bet has been placed, a craps number (Two, Three, or Twelve) comes up, the bet loses. If a Seven or an Eleven is rolled on the first roll after the Come bet has been placed, then the bet wins.

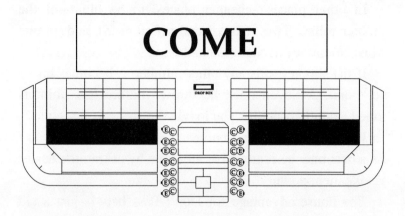

If the first roll of the dice after the bet is placed comes up a Four, Five, Six, Eight, Nine, or Ten, then that becomes the bettor's—but not the shooter's—point, and that number must be rolled again before the Seven is rolled to win.

It is easy to place a Come bet. The Come box is huge. As is true of all bets on the board, pretend that the box you want to place your chips in is a small diagram of your end of the table. You place your chips in the portion of the box that corresponds to the place where you are standing, and that way the dealer will know that it is your bet.

Once the bettor's point has been established, the dealer will move the bettor's bet from the Come box to the adjacent box for the appropriate number.

If you lose, the dealer will remove your chips from the table and you will have to place new chips in the Come Box if you want to bet again.

If you win, the dealer will place twice your original bet on the Come box. If you want to bet nothing or only a part of that it is up to you to remove the chips from the table.

If you do not touch your chips the dealer will assume that you are letting your bet ride, that is, betting all of your winnings. Most betting schemes are just a tad more conservative than that.

Most craps players either bet the same amount all of the time, or they increase their bets depending on the circumstances in pre-planned increments, so they remove all of their winnings except for the amount they want to bet from the Come box after the dealer has paid off.

The house advantage for a Come bet is the same as that for a Pass Line bet: 1.41 percent.

DON'T COME BET

The Don't Come bet is similar to the Don't Pass bet, except that it can only be placed after the shooter has established a

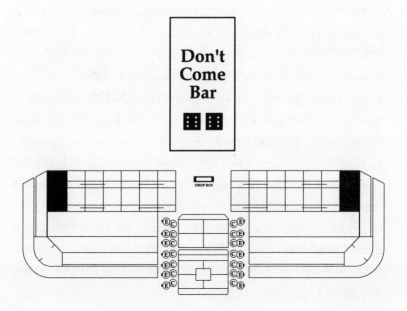

point. You'll notice that the Don't Come box is much smaller than the Come box, because this bet, even though it is slightly smarter than the Come bet is considered "betting to lose." That is *lose* as in losing the game, not losing money.

If the first roll of the dice after the bet is placed is a Two or a Three, you win even money. If the first roll is a Seven or an Eleven, you lose.

If the first roll is a Twelve it is a push—that is, no money exchanges hands. Any other number—the Four, Five, Six, Eight, Nine, and Ten—becomes your point.

Once again, your point but not the shooter's point. The dealer will move the chips from the Come box into the appropriate number box so he won't forget your point.

You are betting that that point will not be made. If the Seven comes up before the point you win even money. If the point is made before a Seven comes up, you lose.

The house advantage on this type of bet is 1.40 percent.

PLACE BETS

To bet that the shooter will roll a specific number—either a Four, Five, Six, Eight, Nine, or Ten—before he rolls a Seven, just tell the dealer you want to make a Place bet on that number. He will Place your bet on the number or numbers of your choice. (You will often hear craps players using the word *place* in Place bets as a verb, as in: "I Placed the Eight for five dollars.")

Players are allowed to make or take off their Place bets at any time they wish. A Place bet on a Four or a Ten pays off at 9–5. A Five or a Nine pays off at 7–5. A Place bet on a Six or an Eight pays off at 7–6.

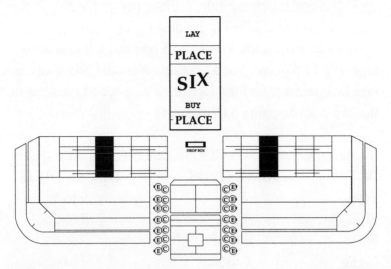

Illustration shows boxes to place chips in if you want to make a Place bet on Six.

If you have placed a bet on the Four and the shooter establishes his point as a Six and then rolls another Six, it is a push, because neither the Four (the number you bet on), nor a Seven has yet come up. No money changes hands.

The shooter now has another Come Out roll. Ordinarily, all Place bets are considered "off" on a Come Out roll unless you tell the dealer that you wish it to be otherwise.

It is also usual casino policy that Place bets must be made in an amount that allows an easy payoff. A Place bet on the Five or the Nine has to be in an amount that is a multiple of five.

A Place bet that is not a multiple of five chips on the Five or the Nine would be very difficult to pay off in chips. A bet of three chips would pay off four and a fifth chips if it won.

Following this same rule, a Place bet on the Six or the Eight has to be made in factors of six.

A Place bet on the Six or the Eight has a house advantage of 1.52 percent. For a Five or a Nine the house advantage is 4 percent. And the vig for a Place bet on the Four or the Ten is a whopping 6.67 percent.

REAL ODDS VERSUS HOUSE ODDS ON PLACE BETS

BET	REAL ODDS	HOUSE ODDS
Four	2 to1	9 to 5
Five	3 to 2	7 to 5
Six	6 to 5	7 to 6
Eight	6 to 5	7 to 6
Nine	3 to 2	7 to 5
Ten	2 to 1	9 to 5

BIG SIX AND BIG EIGHT BETS

Some casinos still offer "Big Six" and "Big Eight" bets, although so many craps players have wised up to this rip-off that many new craps tables have eliminated the betting space from the setup.

The bet was that the Six (or the Eight, depending on which one you bet) would come up before the shooter rolled a Seven. The problem was that Sixes and Eights do not come up as frequently as Sevens. (No number comes up as frequently as the Seven.)

Additionally, the Big Six and Big Eight bet only paid off even money. The house advantage on these bets was astronomical, so much so that they are quickly becoming a thing of the past.

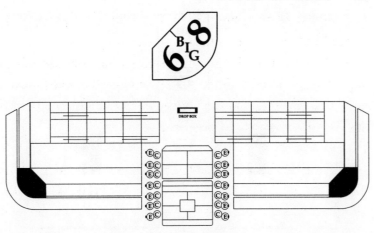

The house advantage for the Big Six and Big Eight bets is a humongous 9.09 percent. So, as Sammy sang in the theme to *Baretta:* "Don't do it, man."

BUY BETS

Buy bets are similar to Place bets, but have slightly different odds. If you want to bet the shooter will roll a Four, Five, Six, Eight, Nine, or Ten before rolling a Seven, just tell the dealer which number you want to buy. The dealer will make the bet for you.

Buy bet minimums are $20 on Four, Five, Nine, or Ten, and $24 if you want to bet on Six or Eight. You must pay a charge (sometimes called a tax) of 5 percent ($1) of the wager to the house at the time you make this bet. You pay the tax because, once the bet is placed, the casino plays fair. They pay off at the true odds. Those odds are 2–1 if you bet on a Four or a Ten, 3–2 when you bet on a Five or a Nine, and 6–5 when you bet on a Six or an Eight.

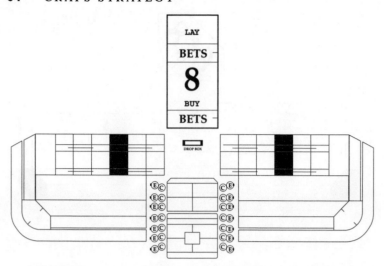

Each Buy bet is on the next roll of the dice only. If your number does not come up and the shooter does not roll a Seven, no money exchanges hands. However, if you say nothing the dealer will assume that you are letting your bet ride. If you want to withdraw your bet, speak up.

You may buy or take off these bets at any time. If you do take off a bet, the 5 percent "tax" is returned to you. However, if the bet is allowed to go to fruition—that is, until the number you bought or a Seven comes up—then the casino will keep the 5 percent regardless of whether you won or lost.

BUYING THE ODDS

When you Buy the Odds you are making the only wager on the table for which the house has no edge. If that's the case, then why doesn't everybody Buy the Odds? Why are other bets so popular?

Well, as usual, the casino can't live in a fair world and they have come up with a way to give themselves an advantage—although a small one compared to the vig of other types of bets.

The rules say that in order to Buy the Odds, you have to make a bet on the Pass Line or in the Come box before you are allowed to Buy the Odds.

In this way, the casino has offered you a bet for which they have no advantage, but you have to make a bet for which they do have an advantage before you can place it.

Still, the miniscule vig when you Buy the Odds makes it the best play on the table.

Once a point has been thrown you may bet up to some multiple, usually two times, your Pass Line bet on the "odds." The odds are simply an additional wager that the point will be rolled before a Seven.

The probability of the point being rolled first is less than 50/50, so, if the point is rolled, you win more than you bet. If the point is a Six or an Eight, the odds pay 6–5.

If the point is a Five or a Nine, the odds pay 3–2.

If the point is a Four or a Ten, the odds pay 2–1.

The multiple you may bet on the odds is usually twice the Pass Line bet for points of Four, Five, Nine, or Ten. That multiple is two and a half times the Pass Line bet when you bet on the Six or the Eight.

The reason you may bet more on a point of Six or Eight is to keep things convenient for the dealers. This way, you can place a $5 Odds bet on top of a $2 Pass Line bet.

A $4 Odds bet on a Six or an Eight would earn the bettor $4.80. That would be awkward since there are no eighty-cent chips on a craps table. The way the rules are, a $5 Odds bet on the Six or Eight wins an even $6.

When casinos first began to offer Odds betting, the rules were that you had to place your Odds bet in the same amount as the Pass Line bet you had already made. This amount is called "single odds."

And there are still casinos in which this is the rule, a fact you should know before playing at a table with the intention of Buying the Odds.

However, the larger the Odds bet becomes the smaller the house advantage becomes. Therefore casinos that were in competition with one another for craps players—such as along the strip in Las Vegas and along the boardwalk in Atlantic City—sweetened the pot by allowing players to bet double their original Pass Line bets as Odds bets.

In these casinos, a $5 Pass Line bet allows a player to make a $10 Odds bet.

In order to place your Odds bet after making a Pass Line bet, you place your chips directly behind your Pass Line bet once a point has been established.

You can also place an Odds bet in addition to a Come bet. To do this you place your chips in the Come box—or, as craps players are apt to say, simply "in the Come"—and, to avoid confusion, you say to the dealer, "Odds on my Come bet."

The dealer will often place your Odds bet directly on top of your Come bet, but slightly out of alignment so that the two bets remain distinguishable.

The higher the Odds bet is in relation to the Pass Line or Come bet that preceded it, the lower the house advantage becomes. However, as you can see from the chart below, the dramatic nature of the decrease stops after ten-times-odds.

COMBINED HOUSE EDGE ON THE PASS LINE AND BUYING ODDS

Here's a chart demonstrating the house edge when you combine the Pass Line and Odds.

one times odds	0.848 percent
two times odds	0.606 percent
full double odds	0.572 percent
three time odds	0.471 percent
five times odds	0.326 percent
10 times odds	0.184 percent
20 times odds	0.099 percent
100 times odds	0.021 percent

LAY BETS

A Lay bet means that you are betting on something that will happen more often than not. To bet that the shooter will *not* roll a Four, Five, Six, Eight, Nine, or Ten before he rolls a Seven, just tell the dealer which number you wish to buy. The dealer will place your bet.

Just as was the case with Buy bets, you must pay a "tax" of five percent of the amount to be won to the House at the time you make this bet. In exchange for that fee, the casino offers payoff odds for Lay bets that are true and correct odds.

Casinos pay off at 1–2—that is, you win $1 for every $2 you bet—when you bet against a Four and a Ten, at 2–3 (bet

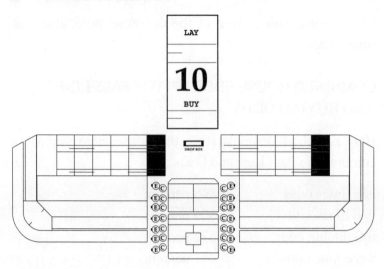

$3 to win $2) when you bet against a Five and a Nine, and at 5–6 on a Six and an Eight.

You may Lay or take off these bets at any time.

If you do take off a bet, the 5 percent charge is returned to you.

Say you place a Lay wager on the Four. There are three ways to roll a Four, yet six ways to make a Seven. Therefore

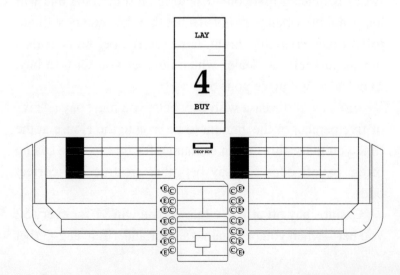

it is twice as likely on every roll of the dice that a Seven will come up than a Four, thus the 1–2 odds.

If you bet $10 and win, you get $15 back—your $10 back plus $5 more. Casinos insist that your bet be an amount that will pay off easily if you win. A $7 bet at 1–2 odds would not be allowed because, if you won, the payoff would be $10.50 and, as we previously discussed, there is no such thing as a fifty-cent chip.

If you place a Lay wager on the Five, the odds are 2–3. That's because there are four ways to make a Five and six ways to make a Seven. Four to six expressed in simplest terms is 2–3. Bet $3 to win $2. Bet $6 to win $4. If you bet $6 and win, you get $10 back. Bet $12 and get back $20, etc.

The odds on the Nine are the same as those on the Five, and the odds on the Ten are the same as those on the Four.

If you place a Lay wager on the Six or the Eight—since there are five ways to make a Six or an Eight and six ways to make a Seven—the odds are 5–6. You bet $6 to win $5,

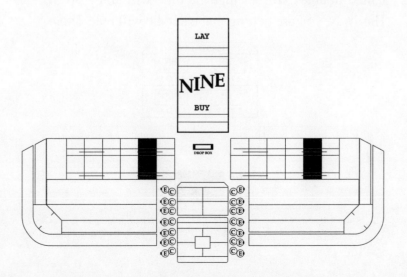

bet $12 to win $10, bet $18 to win $15, etc. Bet $18 and win and you get $33 back. Get it?

The house advantage varies depending on which number you are placing a Lay wager on. Taking into consideration the 5 percent surcharge to place the bet, the house advantage is 4 percent for the Six or Eight; 3.23 percent on the Five or the Nine; and 2.44 percent on the Four or the Ten.

Lay bets are not popular and, with the possible exception of the Four and Ten, the size of the house advantage does not make this type of bet worth your while.

ALL-DAY HARDWAYS

The boxes for these bets are located at the center of the table, directly in front of the position where the boxman sits. Since the "Hardway" area on the table is so far from where the players stand, you give your chips to the stickman and instruct him how you would like them placed on the layout.

A "Hardway," if you were playing Monopoly, would be called doubles. To bet that the dice will come up Six the Hardway, you are betting that each die will read Three.

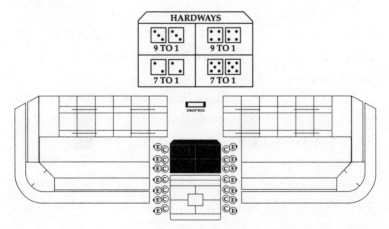

However, when you bet on Six the Hardway, you are betting that it will come up before either the next Seven, or a Six the easy way (any one of the other combinations that add up to six).

You may place Hardway bets on the Four, Six, Eight, and Ten. Each has a true probability of coming up of 35–1 for each roll of the dice.

If you are betting on the Six Hardway, you can be beat by a Seven, which comes up six times for every thirty-six rolls of the dice, and by any of these: Four/Two, Two/Four, One/Five, and Five/One. Those combinations come up four times for every thirty-six rolls.

So, for every one winning roll, on the average, there will be ten losing rolls. That means that the odds of you winning are 10–1, but the bet is only paid off by the casino at 9–1.

When you bet on the Eight Hardway, there is only one dice combination that will win—that is, the Four/Four. However, all six variations of Seven, plus the four ways to roll an Eight the easy way (Six/Two, Two/Six, Five/Three, Three/Five) are losers. Again, the odds are 10–1 that a loser will come up before the winner—yet the payoff is only 9–1.

If you bet on the Four or the Ten Hardway, there is, of course, one way to win, but in these cases there are eight losing combinations. So the odds that you will win are 8–1 yet the casinos only pay off at 7–1.

To bet the Six or the Eight Hardway is to give the casino an astronomical 9.09 percent advantage. To bet the Four or the Ten Hardway is even worse, giving the house an 11.1 percent advantage.

Clearly, you should steer clear of Hardway bets at all times. A one-roll or "Hopping Hardway" is a bet that a specific Hardway number will come up on the next roll of the dice. These bets pay 30–1 (true odds are 35–1) when the number rolls, and you lose if any other number rolls.

PROPOSITION BETS

Proposition bets—sometimes called one-roll bets—are bets on the outcome on the next roll of the dice, and the next roll only. They are placed in the center of the layout and are under the domain of the stickman rather than the dealers.

These are not popular bets, especially with experienced craps players, because the house advantage is so extreme that it is very difficult to turn a profit there. However, sometimes craps players do play hunches and the Proposition bet section does not go entirely unused.

Since most players are off to the sides of the craps table, cozying up to their nearest dealer, it is often necessary to toss your chips in the general direction of the center of the table when you want to place a Proposition bet and then verbally instruct the stickman where to put your chips.

If you place your bet on the "Any Craps" section in the Proposition bets section at the center of the layout, you are betting that a Two, Three, or Twelve will be rolled on the next roll of the dice.

Since there is only one way to roll a Two, one way to roll a Twelve, and two ways to roll a Three, there are four winning combinations out of a possible thirty-six results. That means that the odds are 8–1. But the casino only pays 7–1. That translates into an advantage to the house of 11.1 percent.

Another Proposition bet is to wager that a Three or Eleven will come up on the next roll. The chances of a Three are two in thirty-four or 17–1. But the casino only pays off at 15–1. The house advantage on such a bet is 11.1 percent.

There is also a square to bet that a Seven will come up on the next roll. As we know, the odds say that a Seven will come up, on the average, once every six rolls of the dice (5–1), but the casino only pays off at 4–1 for this bet. That translates into a 16.67 percent advantage to the house.

You might as well just drop the cash in the toilet and start flushing.

You can also bet that a Two (snake eyes) or a Twelve (boxcars) will come up on the next roll. Although we can easily figure out that there is one chance in thirty-six of rolling a Two or a Twelve (35–1), the casino only pays off at 30–1. That translates into a hefty house advantage of 13.89 percent.

FIELD BET

A Field bet is on the next roll of the dice only. If the shooter rolls a Two or a Twelve, you are paid off at a rate of 2–1. If a Three, Four, Nine, Ten, or Eleven is rolled, you win even

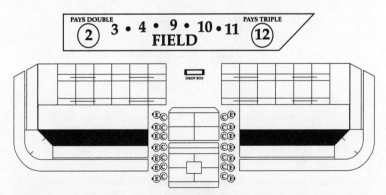

To make a Field bet, place chips in the box below, which is located between the Come bar and the Pass Line.

money. If any other number comes up, you lose the bet. The house advantage for a Field bet is 2.78 percent.

HORN BET

Another Proposition bet is called the Horn bet. That means you are betting that the shooter will roll either Two, Three, Eleven, or Twelve.

The Horn bet, for reasons we will discover, has been called "making four bad bets all at once."

Sure, if the shooter rolls any of these numbers, you win. Each Horn bet is for one roll of the dice only. If you say nothing, the dealer will assume that you are letting your bet ride.

To place a Horn bet you throw your chips in the general direction of the stickman and say something zesty like: "Around the Horn!"

Because you are betting on all four numbers simultaneously, you must make a bet that is divisible by four. The

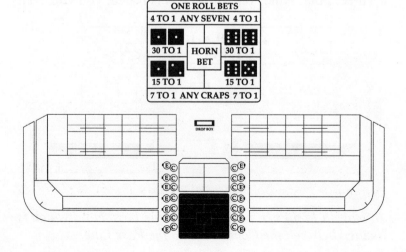

stickman will then divide your bet four ways and place an equal amount on the Two, Three, Eleven, or Twelve.

The problem with this bet is that you are automatically placing three losing bets. That's because, if, say, a Twelve is thrown on the next roll of the dice, you win 29–1 or $150 (which includes the $5 you bet on the Twelve), when the real probability of that happening is 35–1.

Plus, your other three $5 bets automatically lose, so your return on your $20 investment is $135, or 6¾-1.

A Two coming up on the first roll of the dice following a Horn bet would have the same outcome. When the Two or the Twelve comes up on a Horn bet, the house advantage is 16.67 percent.

If the Three or the Eleven comes up, the bet pays off at 14–1 on your $5 bet. Once again, the problem is that you actually bet $20. When a Three or an Eleven comes up on a Horn bet, the house advantage is also 16.67 percent.

Con men scour casinos looking for people who like to place Horn bets because they are apt to buy anything—like maybe a few hundred acres of swampland in Florida.

HARDWAYS: THEY'RE GOOD FOR SOMETHING

Although the Hardways and the Proposition bets are strictly for suckers only, they do have their place in craps culture. They are routinely used to tip the crew.

If you want to tip your dealer, you do it by placing a bet for him in the center section of the table. If the bet loses, no big deal. If it wins, then you have given your dealer a nice tip.

ON THE TURN

An "On the Turn" bet is another one-roll bet that may be made on any specific combination of the dice from Four through Ten with the exception of the Hardways.

Out of every thirty-six rolls of the dice, this should be accomplished twice, but these bets only pay 15–1 (actual odds 17–1) when the specified combination rolls, and they lose if any other number or combination rolls.

HOUSE ADVANTAGES (IN PERCENTAGES)

Pass Line: 1.41%

Come: 1.41%

Don't Pass: 1.40%

Don't Come: 1.40%

Place bet on Six or Eight: 1.515%

Place bet on Five or Nine: 4.000%

Place bet on Four or Ten: 6.667%

Place bet to lose on Six or Eight: 1.818%

Place bet to lose on Five or Nine: 2.500%

Place bet to lose on Four or Ten: 3.030%

Buy bet on Six or Eight: 4.762%

Buy bet on Five or Nine: 4.762%

Buy bet on Four or Ten: 4.762%

Lay bet to lose on Six or Eight: 4.000%

Lay bet to lose on Five or Nine: 3.226%

Lay bet to lose on Four or Ten: 2.439%

Big Six/Big Eight: 9.091%

Hard Four/Hard Ten: 11.111%

Hard Six/Hard Eight: 9.091%.

Craps Two/Craps Twelve:13.889%

Craps Three/Craps Eleven: 11.111%

Any Craps: 11.111% Any Seven: 16.667%

Horn (Eight a Two or a Twelve): 12.500%

Field: 2.778%.

HOUSE ADVANTAGES (IN ODDS)

Bet	True Odds	House Odds
Any Seven	5 to 1	4 to 1
Any Craps (Two, Three, or Twelve)	8 to 1	7 to 1
Two	35 to 1	30 to 1
Twelve	35 to 1	30 to 1
Three	17 to 1	15 to 1
Eleven	17 to 1	15 to 1

CALLING BETS OFF

There are some bets you may take off the table while the game is underway—but only before the dice rolls. Bets you can remove are:

- the Odds bet behind your Pass Line bet.
- the Odds bet on top of your Come bets on the numbers. (You cannot remove a Pass Line or a Come bet that is on a number at any time.)

- a Don't Pass bet.
- and Don't Come bet.
- any Place bet on a number.

To call a bet off, you have to tell the dealer and get his confirmation that he heard you. If the dealer did not hear you, then your bet counts.

SUMMARY

So what have we learned? We have learned that betting on the Pass Line (betting with the shooter) and the Don't Pass Line (betting against the shooter), while either taking or laying the odds are the smartest bets in craps.

If, on the first or Come Out roll, the shooter does not roll Two, Three, Seven, Eleven, or Twelve, he has "a point." If he rolls this number again before he rolls a Seven, he wins.

The odds against rolling this number before a Seven vary depending on what the point is. Let's say the shooter rolls a Four on his first roll. To win, he now needs another Four before he rolls a Seven.

There are six combinations of dice that add up to Seven: Four-Three, Three-Four, Five-Two, Two-Five, Six-One, and One-Six. Only three combinations of the dice will give you a sum of Four: Three-One, One-Three, and Two-Two.

For each roll of the dice, it is twice as likely that a Seven will be rolled as it is that a Four will be rolled. The odds are 2–1. If you have bet the Pass Line and another player opens with a Four, you can back up your Pass Line bet with an amount equal to your original wager.

Now, if the player rolls a Four before a Seven, you win your original bet plus twice your back-up bet. The house pays you 2-1, which are the true odds.

For Don't Pass bettors, the converse applies. Using the same example, after making your initial bet that the roller will not make his point and the roller establishes that point as a Four, you can make a second wager equal in amount to the first just as you did before, but, since it is twice as likely that you will win as lose, you must lay the true odds.

That is, you must bet $2 to win $1, $4 to win $2, $8 to win $4, etc. The Odds bets in craps are the only even-money bet in the entire casino.

Each "point" pays different odds:

POINT	ODDS
Four	2–1
Five	3–2
Six	6–5
Eight	6–5
Nine	3–2
Ten	2–1

The house retains a small advantage even with these even-money bets because you are not allowed to place them unless you have first placed a bet of the equal amount on the Pass or Don't Pass Line, both bets for which the casino retains an advantage.

Some casinos will allow you to reduce your disadvantage even closer to zero by betting twice the amount of your original bet on the Odds bet.

Keep in mind that betting against the shooter gives you a slightly greater chance of winning than betting with the shooter, but it is also not a great way to meet people and make friends.

Since most players at any given craps table are going to be betting with the shooter, your Don't Pass bet will be construed as antisocial and possibly even an attempt to jinx the shooter and those that are betting in his favor.

CHEATING

There is a way of thinking that says it is indeed not immoral to cheat at dice when playing in a casino because the game is rigged against you, and if they can cheat, you can cheat as well.

Besides, the thinking goes, it isn't a person you are ripping off, but a money-sucking conglomerate, so where's the harm? (The harm, by the way, is that this is a game and by cheating you are taking the fun out it.)

SLIDERS

The most common form of cheating involves teamwork. One of the conspirators is the shooter of the dice, while the others are players around the table.

The players all call in late bets in an effort to simultaneously distract the boxman and each member of the crew. The shooter, sensing the moment when no eyes are on him, throws the dice, but instead of rolling the dice—bouncing them so that they go this way and that, turning over many times before coming to a stop—the dice mechanic, as they are called, slides the dice down the table, so that they end up with the same numbers on top as they had when the shooter held them in his hand.

Usually the shooter will position himself directly to the left of the stickman, while a key conspirator will position himself to the right of the stickman, distracting his attention away from the shooter.

Since the system is not perfect—all rolls of the dice are supposed to strike the wall and a slider has to keep his dice off the wall for his technique to work, and every once in a while a crew member watches a mechanic doing his thing—the cheating shooter has learned to spin the dice as he slides them, so that they are a blur as they move along the table.

An experienced gang of cheaters will also be aware of when the shifts change, so that they are dealing with a tired and bored crew, one that is about to get off for the night. This crew is much less likely to be razor-sharp and looking for improprieties.

A crew that is near the end of its shift probably isn't paying nearly as close attention to the manner in which the shooter is shooting the dice as a brand-new, fresh crew would be, because they have one eye on their watch.

While it is true that this scheme would be uncovered soon enough if they tried to do it again and again at the same table, that is not their *modus operandi*. They come in, invade a table, play until their shooter gets the dice, do their thing for one big hit, and then they split.

They move on to another table, or even more likely to another casino, never staying at one place long enough for casino personnel to catch on to what they are doing.

I do not want to imply by using the pronoun "he," that all cheaters are men. On the contrary, women are among the best "sliders," and, as co-conspirators, they are even more effective than men at distracting male crew members.

If you are a craps dealer and you want to look out for cheaters, here are some things you should be aware of:

1) Take note of the shooter in any situation in which there seems to be a rush of last-second activity before the dice are thrown.

2) Beware of any shooter who bends down over the table when picking up the dice and takes an unusually long time holding the dice before releasing them. The slider has to get down over the table so that he can release the dice right upon the table's surface. Also, he needs to put the correct sides up before he releases so that his throw will get the desired results.

SPIN DOCTORS

For those who want to stick around at one table for more than one quick hit, cheaters have developed the spin shot. This isn't to be confused with the spinning slide. Those dice spin on one face. Here we are talking about dice that bounce and turn like normally thrown dice, but only along a single axis.

Those who spin the dice in this fashion cannot absolutely predict the outcome of each of their throws. But, by determining which axis the dice will spin on, they have taken two sets of two numbers out of play and thus have made the game far more predictable.

Spinners say that they hold the dice tightly pressed together with their pinky and thumb. They spin the dice with their fore-, second-, and ring-fingers.

Although it is far more difficult to distinguish a spinner as a cheater than it would be if he were a slider, spinners also avoid bouncing the dice off the wall, and this will attract attention.

If a die is being rolled along the axis that goes through its Two and its Five, then it will end up settling with the Six, Four, One, or Three up. The Two and the Five will remain on the sides.

Personally, I do not have the soul of a cheater, so none of this is of great interest to me. I think that the fear of losing is what makes the joy of winning that much more intense.

Fix the game and it isn't gambling anymore, is it?

What happens to a mechanic if he gets caught cheating? That varies from casino to casino. A lot of casinos do not want cheaters at their craps tables, but the idea of cheaters at their competitors' craps tables does not displease them that much.

Therefore, they concentrate their efforts on identifying the cheaters and banning them from the premises. Other, more morally upstanding casinos will call the police and have the cheaters arrested for attempting to "steal" casino money.

Some stickmen, if they see a cheater, will merely "accidentally" put their stick in front of the dice as they are sliding, causing "no roll" to be called.

The shooter, knowing that the stickman is on to him, will usually discontinue his cheating and probably will move to a new casino without any fuss.

CHAPTER THREE
STRATEGIES FOR WINNING

What follows are the true-life stories of twenty individuals who have used various craps strategies to increase their chances of winning. Some have improved by changing where and when they place their bets. Others have altered their money-management techniques to turn things for the better.

So here are the stories of the winners, and from each there is (at least) one lesson to be learned.

CASE HISTORY #1

JONATHAN L.: Learning to Love Laying the Odds

Jonathan L. is a thirty-seven-year-old bachelor who works on Wall Street. On his weekends he enjoys going to the casinos of Atlantic City to shoot dice.

"I guess that working in stocks and bonds makes me a natural gambler," says Jonathan.

Until recently, Jonathan admits, he lost a lot more than he won. But, using a new strategy, Jonathan has turned his luck around at the craps table. I'll let him explain:

"I was always betting the longshot bets, because I liked the thrill of the big hit, even though it didn't happen very often—certainly not often enough to make the wait worth my while.

"I decided to change my entire tack at the table. Instead of betting the possibilities that were the least likely to happen, I switched and began to bet those that were most likely to happen.

"Now, instead of betting the Hardways, I tell the dealer to, say, lay the Four. I give him fifty dollars in chips, plus one for the house, and he places my chips in the back of the Four box with a marker that says 'lay' lying on top.

"In other words, I am betting that the shooter is going to roll a Seven before he rolls a Four. Over the long run, you know, there should be exactly twice as many Sevens as Fours rolled.

"If I win, and I usually do as the odds would indicate, I get my fifty dollars back, plus twenty-five dollars more. If I lose, of course, I am out the fifty dollars. It is possible, because the odds are so strongly in my favor, to get on some tremendous hot streaks, unlike anything I had ever experienced when I insisted on betting the longest shots on the table.

"Psychologically, it is difficult for some people to place a bet in which they can lose more than they can win. But that is really silly because they are betting on an occurrence that is so much more likely to happen.

"Another psychological boundary that many players have to overcome is the fact that you have to win more than you lose to break even. If a player who is laying the odds wins three times and loses three times he is losing big, and yet he may not feel like he is losing, since he has been collecting on half of his bets.

"Another great reason to play this way is that it is fair, or at least as close to fair as the casinos will allow. On the longshot bets the house inevitably pays much less than you really deserve.

"With the exception of the chip you pay to the house when you make the bet, laying the odds is a precisely fair payoff—and that's something that is hard to find in a casino no matter where you are playing.

"And it's funny, because I have made a similar strategy switch on Wall Street recently. With the recent troubles in the stock market, I didn't make a whole lot by playing conservatively, but I avoided losing my shirt, which is more than I can say for some of my wilder colleagues."

CASE HISTORY #2

JENNIFER G.: Placing the Six or Eight

Jennifer G. is a twenty-six-year-old flight attendant who works for a major commercial airline. She is originally from Troy, New York, but currently lives in Los Angeles.

"I have overnight stays in Las Vegas quite a bit, so naturally I go the casinos," she says.

After playing the slots for a while, and a brief stint at the blackjack table, Jennifer found her true love: Craps.

"Even to this day, I can't wait until it is my turn to roll the dice," she says excitedly.

The trouble was, Jennifer, for all of her love of the game, was not making any money.

"I had no real strategy. I played whatever I felt like playing. I had myself convinced that it was an intuitive game, that if I allowed my brain to go blank, I would be able to correctly predict who was going to make their point and who wasn't. Then I happened upon a system that works for me. I understand that there are books about it, but truth is, I learned it from a friend."

Jennifer is correct about the books. The best book about her system is called *Advantage Craps* by Roger L. Ford.

"The system goes like this. I start by placing my bets on the Six or Eight. I do this either right after the Come Out roll by a new shooter, after the previous shooter has Sevened out; or, after a Seven has been rolled on a Come Out roll, any Come Out roll.

"Since the chances of rolling a Six or an Eight are five in thirty-six, and the chances of rolling a Seven are six in thirty-six, there is a slightly greater chance that I will lose than win, so I place that bet immediately following a Seven—or, if a Seven has been rolled since the last Six or Eight.

"Sometimes that second option is necessary because you have to wait until the shooter has made her point before you can place the bet.

"If there is a new shooter and he rolls Six as his point, I do not place a bet on the Six or Eight and I won't until after the next Seven has been rolled. But, if the point is anything other than a Six or an Eight—that is, a Ten, Nine, Five, or Four, then I place the bet.

"I bet in three stages. You may be a higher roller than I am—I play at the dollar tables they have along the Strip— so any multiples of these numbers work the same.

"I start out betting three dollars each—for you it could be thirty dollars or three hundred dollars—on the Six and Eight when a Seven has been rolled since the last Six or Eight.

"Whenever I bet on the Six and Eight and lose, I increase my next wager to the next level, which is six dollars each—or sixty dollars, or six hundred dollars for you.

"If I win, I immediately tell the dealer to take my bets on the Six and Eight down. I don't want him to think that I am letting my bets ride because I am not.

"After I win I revert to my smallest bet. At least I say I do, and that is the smartest thing to do, but the truth of the matter is that I see craps as a streaky game and I am apt to keep my bet at the maximum if it looks like I am going to win a couple of times in a row.

"The danger of that is that a loss can hurt you more than the system is designed for it to. By the same token, if I feel that the table is getting cold and the Sevens are starting to come in bunches, I will sit out for a while, waiting for the tide to turn before starting again with three dollars on the Six and three dollars on the Eight when a Seven has been rolled since the last Six or Eight.

"My rule of thumb is that I never, ever allow myself to lose three times in row. If I have been beaten by the Seven twice in a row, I let one opportunity to bet go by before I place my bets again.

"Since I have started this method I have won much more frequently. Having a strong, defined game plan has also allowed me to stay focused at the table.

"I think I used to become rather mechanized at the table, making the same bet over and over again and then, oops, where did all of my chips go?

"That does not happen to me anymore, I can assure you. The beauty of the scheme is that it works even on a table that is not terribly hot. After all, I bet the Six or Eight regardless of what the shooter's point is."

CASE HISTORY #3

RODNEY G.: Placing the Six or Eight, Part II

Rodney G. is a forty-seven-year-old C.P.A. who routinely takes a long vacation during the late spring and early summer—just after what accountants call "tax season." (Rodney is a friend of Jennifer G.'s, in our previous case history, which explains his references to her.)

"I'll fess up. I'm the guy who told Jennifer about the Advantage system. I used the system—and quite successfully, too—for a long time, but I found that the system had one problem, at least as far as I was concerned: It was boring.

"Like many craps players, I am a little dazzled by craps. Craps feels like a perpetual machine with many moving—and busy!—parts. When I played the system I felt as if there was a big world out there and I was restricting myself to a small corner of it.

"I wanted to have fun but I didn't want to be foolish. So now I use a variation on the system that Jennifer told you about, but one I find just a tad more exciting, at least in the sense that it allows you to join in on the camaraderie when a table gets hot.

"Jennifer's system calls for placing the Six and Eight only in situations when a Seven has been rolled since either of those numbers.

"In my strategy, I place bets on the Six and Eight only when a Six or Eight has been rolled since the last time there was a Seven rolled.

"If a shooter rolls a Six or Eight on the Come Out roll, that counts, too. And then, as soon as one of those numbers hit, you ask the dealer to take down your bets. Then you wait until the next time a Six or an Eight are rolled and immediately tell the dealer to place the Six and Eight.

"In this way you get to root for the Six or the Eight to come up when, most of the time, those numbers are the shooter's point. Therefore you tend to win when the shooter wins and lose when the shooter loses, which I think is a lot more fun because you get to share in the excitement of a hot table.

"I also bet progressively—usually fifty, one hundred, two hundred—starting at the minimum and moving up a level each time I lose, staying at the top level until I win and then reverting back to the lowest level.

"That's the way it goes unless I lose three or four times in a row. When that happens I pick up my chips and go for a stroll. A little bit of a stroll for my luck to change, and then I try again—only this time at a different table."

CASE HISTORY #4

EDWARD B.: Learning to walk away

Eddie B. is a retired C.P.A. who breeds Thoroughbred race horses. Next to going to the farm to see a new foal, his true love is craps. But it wasn't until recently that Eddie began to walk away from craps tables with more chips than he started with.

His "strategy" has more to do with his psychological approach to the game rather than upon what and how much he bets.

Eddie says, "For years I lost a lot more often than I won when I played craps, and there was a simple reason: Whenever I got ahead I told myself that I was 'playing with their money,' and I would start to go wild.

"Since, as I told myself, I had 'nothing to lose,' I took chances that I shouldn't have taken and it wouldn't be long before that hundred dollars was gone and I was out of the black and into the red.

"In other words, the only time I thought about quitting was when I was behind. I wasn't always behind by a great deal, but the truth was that that particular stint at the craps table had been a negative rather than a positive one.

"Then I realized that, during most of my periods of play, there was one time when I was ahead, usually by some decent amount. If I could learn to quit at that moment each time I would win far more often than I lost, for I would only lose on those times when I was never ahead.

"So, instead of setting a sky-high figure for my *walk-away point*—that is the amount of money I would have to be ahead before I cashed in, I made my walkaway point more reasonable. Say, a hundred dollars.

"That is, every time I am a hundred dollars ahead, I stop playing. I may come back in an hour or later that night and play again, but right then and there I am done. And the next time I start playing, I start again at zero.

"That way I got away from that 'I'm playing with their money' mentality. I found that more often than not, there was a time when I was a hundred dollars ahead, and each of those times I made a hundred dollars at the craps table.

Some players use little psychological tricks to make it easier for them to quit when they are ahead. Eddie would pretend that he was in a tournament in which the object of the game was to get to $100 ahead. When he reached that magic number he would inwardly celebrate because he had 'won' the contest. First prize, so to speak, was a hundred dollars.

"It doesn't always work," Eddie admits. "There are going to be days when you get to ninety-five dollars ahead and then start to slide, and you never get that far ahead again. So, like all craps strategies, this one is not perfect, but one thing is for sure. I win now a lot more than I used to—and I am having a lot more fun playing, too."

CASE HISTORY #5

THOMAS D.: Setting a loss limit

Thomas D. works for a Missouri-based insurance company and enjoys visiting the riverboat casinos near St. Louis on his weekends. Like Eddie in the previous case history, Tom

increased his winnings at craps by setting limits, by desig-
nating ahead of time when he would walk away from the
table. His self-set limit, however, concerned the amount he
was willing to lose rather than win during any single stretch
of craps play.

"I found that, because I am a conservative player and I
usually have a pretty sound strategy behind my play, that I
win more often than I lose. But, over the long run, I was
still down money at the craps tables. That was because I
was losing a lot when I lost and winning only marginally
when I won. The key for me to make money, I eventually
figured out, was to set a limit on the amount I lost.

Unlike Eddie, Tom would never set a limit on the
amount he won.

"I do, however, have a feel for when my luck has peaked
and things are starting to go the other way, so I have always
been good at quitting while I am ahead. My problem is that
I hate to lose so much that I am slow to admit that I have
lost. Because of that I would throw bad money after good
and continue to lose—even after it was clear to everyone
except me that the dice, for me, were running icy cold.

"But this is no longer a problem for me because I have
set a numerical figure which I will not go below. When I am
down that particular number—usually two hundred and
fifty dollars—I quit."

As in the previous case history, Tom may come back
later in the day or night and play again, but when he does he
once again starts at zero.

If he wins, he tries to keep winning. If he loses, he waits
until his losses once again get to the magic number and he
quits. Tom still wins more often than he loses and when he

wins his winnings are usually still marginal. The one thing that has changed is that, whereas he used to have major disasters when he lost, his losing sessions are no longer a big deal and in this way Tom has gone from being a losing craps player to being a winner.

Although it isn't the case with either Eddie or Tom, many craps players set walkaway limits for both winning and losing.

CASE HISTORY #6

STEPHANIE T.: "Three-four-five times odds"

Stephanie T. is a thirty-two-year-old Boulder, Colorado, real estate agent who travels to Las Vegas to play craps every chance she gets.

"I became a winner at craps when I discovered 'three-four-five' times odds," Stephanie says. "I don't think that there is a better bet on the table and I've had some terrific hot streaks since I started playing it."

As we learned earlier, one-times odds means that your Odds bet is equal in amount to the bet you have placed on the Pass Line or in the Come box.

Recall that the casino pays honest odds for Odds bets— but there is a hitch. They only offer this bet to a player who has already placed an equally large Pass Line or Come bet.

Two-times odds means that you are allowed to place an Odds bet that is twice the size of the Come or Pass Line bet. Because the only bet upon which the house has an advantage stays the same in size, the larger the Odds bet, the smaller the house advantage. Competing casinos often attempt to attract customers by offering larger Odds bets. Stephanie found a casino that offered a great deal—and she has turned that discovery into profits.

"With 'three-four-five times odds,'" Stephanie says, "the player can take three-times odds on the Four and Ten; four-times odds on the Five and Nine, and five-times odds on the Six and Eight.

"I play a four-tiered betting scheme, starting at ten dollars and progressing up to fifty dollars a roll, always increasing my bet with a loss and retreating to the base level bet after a win," Stephanie explains.

Assuming the player takes the maximum allowable odds, the payoff on any Odds bet will conveniently always be six times the Pass or Come bet. So Stephanie is correct when she says that it is one of the better bets on the table. The combined house edge under these rules is an extremely tempting 0.37 percent.

"The only problem with playing my system is that you just can't do it in every casino. The three-four-five is available only in areas where casinos are extremely competitive with one another," Stephanie says. "In fact, as far as I know, it is only available at some casinos in Vegas. If I find myself in Connecticut or along the Gulf Shore or in Atlantic City, I have to find another system to play—usually exploiting whatever the best Odds Bets they offered was. But that usually threw me off my game. My recommendation would be for every player to find out what the best Odds bets are at that casino. And, if you are in Las Vegas, I would keep looking until I found a place that had three-four-five."

CASE HISTORY #7

CHARLIE F.: Upside Money Management

Charlie F. had a common problem when he played craps.

"I had trouble figuring out when my hot streak was over, and I would end up giving all of the money I won back to the house. My play would cool off and by the time I realized it, all of my profits were gone," says Charlie, a fifty-four-year-old talent agent who frequently provides talent to the casinos both in the desert and along the East Coast.

"On the other hand, I like to play too much to quit after five minutes. If I start out on a hot streak and win a bundle right off the bat, some systems would have me walk away right then and there. I guess that strategy is okay if you are playing craps for money only, but if you enjoy the game you are bound to feel disappointed even if you are up a large amount."

Then Charlie discovered something called Upside Money Management, and it worked for him.

"In order to walk away from the table with as much money as possible," Charlie says, "I decide beforehand how much winnings I will be satisfied with.

"Let's keep the math simple. If I buy a hundred dollars worth of chips, I tell myself before I even place my first bet that I will be satisfied if I walk away up three hundred dollars."

There are those who say you should never limit your winnings—but, as we have seen, there are also those who have trouble quitting any game when they are ahead.

Here's how Charlie's system works: "If I am up the three hundred dollars—that is, I have a total of four hundred dollars in chips in front of me including the one hundred dollars worth of chips I started out with—it means I am winning, and may be on a hot streak. Some systems would have me quit here because I have reached my goal.

"But instead, I want to keep playing. I like playing craps even when I am not on a hot streak. When the table is burning up for me, the last thing I want to do is quit—so I don't.

"I put three hundred fifty dollars aside—this is money I 'lock up'—and continue to play with the other fifty dollars. If I lose the fifty dollars, that means that my hot streak is over and I walk away with my winnings. I am still up two hundred fifty dollars, after all.

"If you are a high roller and these numbers seem like chump change to you, feel free to add as many zeros as you like to each number. The concept is the same no matter what league you are playing in.

"If I continue to win—say I win another hundred dollars, so now I have a total of five hundred dollars in chips in front of me—then I 'lock up' four hundred dollars, and continue to play with the remaining hundred dollars. If I drop back down to the money I have locked up, I walk away! Without hesitation. Done. This takes great discipline, but I do it."

The basic idea behind Charlie's "up-side" strategy is once he has attained his initial goal, he continues playing and could continue winning—but only with a small portion of his *winnings* at risk.

The remainder of his winnings—the majority of his profits, in other words—becomes untouchable. As his winnings continue to grow, at some point the tide changes and he begins to lose.

"The idea is to quit playing when you have dropped ten to twenty percent from the most you were up beyond attaining your initial goal," Charlie concludes.

CASE HISTORY #8

CONSTANCE Q: The Classic Regression

Constance Q. is a forty-seven-year-old executive in the music industry. After many years of playing craps, she has come up with a system that works for her.

"I always start every session at the craps table by placing a five dollar bet on the Pass Line," Constance says. "After a few of those I begin to place Odds bets, and I do so by following these rules:

"If the shooter had already established his point, and it is a Four or a Ten, I place Single Odds on the point. That is, I bet an additional five dollars.

"If, on the other hand, the shooter has established his point as a Five or a Nine, I place six dollars behind the Pass Line. If the point is a Six or an Eight, I place ten dollars, or double odds, behind the Pass Line. After a few rounds of this I have a feel for the flow of the table and I am ready to start my real system.

"My goal is to make a profit on one victory. So, I wait until the shooter has made his point. After the point has been established, and regardless of what the point is, I place Double Odds, that is six dollars on the Pass Line and twelve dollars on both the Six and the Eight.

"I leave the Double Odds bet up until I win, at which point I tell the dealer to reduce each bet to Single Odds. I am now two dollars up and I can no longer lose if the shooter throws a Seven.

"After I win another time with the Single Odds bets in place, I ask the dealer to take down all of my bets. I then wait for the shooter to make his point, or Seven out, whichever he is going to do.

"I then start the whole procedure over again. Since there are ten different ways for the dice to come up either showing Six or Eight, but only six ways to make a Seven, I should win more than I lose. Do not bet the Six or the Eight, however. Always bet them both."

CASE HISTORY #9

TONY C.: Three-Point Molly

Tony C. is a forty-three-year-old horse claimer from Yonkers, New York.

"I live in a harness-racing town but I claim Thoroughbreds," Tony explains. His youngest daughter is named Nyra, after the New York Racing Association.

Tony plays most of his craps in illegal, sometimes floating, games in the Bronx, more often than not in private clubs. But Tony has also been known to visit both the Indian reservations of Connecticut and the A.C. Boardwalk.

"I used to bop around from scheme to scheme when it came to craps betting," Tony said. "I used to believe whatever I was told. It took me a while before I realized that casinos are a hotbed for tall tales.

"Craps players are a lot like fishermen. They have many stories and almost none of them are true. Just as every fisherman has a story about the largest fish they've ever caught—and usually the largest fish that got away—craps players are filled with stories of the time they held the dice for a half hour while they made pass after pass, or the time they bet on boxcars five times in a row, each time letting their winnings ride, until they walked out with twenty-four million dollars.

"Before you congratulate them, realize that the odds against rolling five consecutive Twelves is closer to sixty million to one. This is also an excellent illustration of how large the house advantage is on this type of bet. The odds that the one time the five straight Twelves came up, there would also be a bettor dumb enough to bet each and every one of them, put this story in the realm of 'can't happen.'

"So, beware before you act out any strategies based on word of mouth information. Wild craps stories can be a lot of fun, but they often lack both truth and logic.

"Then, contrary to everything I just said, I finally heard of a betting strategy at craps that made so much sense that I tried it and once I tried it I have stuck with it ever since."

The simple strategy that Tony learned of is called "Three-Point Molly," and it has turned his craps game around.

"I find that I go home a winner more often than not while using it," Tony says.

The trick to "Three-Point Molly" is to have three numbers working for you at all times. It involves having a Pass Line bet and two Come bets working simultaneously.

"Here's the way it goes," Tony explains. "First, you make a Pass Line bet. You then back up your Pass Line bet with Single or Double Odds.

"Next, you make a Come Line bet. As you did with your Pass Line bet, you back up each Come bet with Single or Double Odds. Two Come bets are the maximum.

"When one of your Come bets wins, place another Come bet. Continue this process until the shooter makes his point or Sevens out.

"The secret behind the system is that, each time you make a Come bet you are protecting your Pass Line bets and taking advantage of a hot roller."

CASE HISTORY #10

NATHAN D.: Anything but Seven

Nathan D. is a twenty-nine-year-old stockbroker who works on Wall Street and does his recreational gambling along the New Jersey shore.

"Ever since I was a little boy I have been a gambler. I enjoy a risk and I like to win," Nathan says. "But that does not mean that I am crazy, and I don't do wacky things.

"Luckily, I have a little knowledge of mathematics and I can figure odds and probabilities in my head fairly rapidly. In other words, I am a quick study when it comes to determining a bad bet from a good bet.

"Even when I am representing my clients on Wall Street I do not go out on the limb too much. I prefer a safer and steadier growth of income, rather than one that may go sky high one day but Geronimo the next. So, as you may have gathered, my betting scheme is fairly conservative.

"Of course, it is my theory that any betting scheme, in order to have any chance of winning over the long run, is going to have to be pretty conservative. People who live by the sword die by the sword, so I never bring my sword to the casino.

"My goal is to win on any number thrown except the Seven. I know that, even though the Seven is more likely to come up than any other number, it is also true that, on any given roll of the dice, it is more likely that a number other than the Seven will come up.

"I do not place any bets on the Don't Pass or Pass Line, but rather I wait until a point has been established. At that time I place two dollars on the Five, Six, and Eight, and one dollar on the Field.

"Since the average roller rolls the dice five times before rolling a Seven, I should make money over the long haul. Since it is never a good idea to press one's luck, I always bring the bets down after three wins rather than bet on a fourth consecutive non-Seven.

"Then I wait until the next point has been established and I start over again," Nathan explains.

CASE HISTORY #11

JUNE R.: Keeping Records

June R. is a fifty-seven-year-old housewife from the south shore of New Jersey. Now that her kids are all away at school, she and her husband enjoy going to Atlantic City on weekends.

"I am a homemaker now," June says. "But I used to be a bookkeeper—and I think the bookkeeper in me has saved me hundreds of dollars at the craps table," she says.

June keeps track of every one of her stints at a craps table. If she plays for an hour in the morning and then for another hour after lunch, she records that as two stints, and enters the figures for each stint individually.

For each stint she records the date, the time of day, her stake, her walk, her net win or loss, and the betting pattern she used.

"My girlfriends call me a craps nerd," says June. "But I don't care. Keeping records has made all the difference for me. I used to have a difficult time sticking to my game plan.

"I would go into a round at the table with a sound plan in mind, but I would get caught up in the emotion of the table, and allow myself to be influenced by what other players were doing, players who are not as good at craps as I am! I also leave space at the side of my chart for other comments. I note the table minimum.

"I write down descriptions of the crew, in case I want to seek out—or avoid—that table and/or personnel in the future. I don't restrict my record keeping to my wins and losses, but also the intangibles."

What did June learn through her record keeping?

"I found out that I do better when I play conservatively," she says. "My records clearly indicated that I had a better chance of winning when I was playing on a twenty-five dollars table as I did when I was playing at a five dollars table. And the reason was clear: when I am playing at the more expensive table I have a strong and healthy fear of losing, and that tends to make me do the right thing."

Of course, you may have a different undiscovered idiosyncrasy when you play, a quirk in your play that may be costing you money, and can be discovered only when you keep detailed records.

CASE HISTORY #12

PETER D.: Stop Worrying About Comps

There are a lot of craps players who will tell you, with a straight face, that the "real way" to make money at a casino is to qualify for all of the complimentary stuff they offer to "high rollers."

They will brag about all of the things they got for free. They received: Free room. Free meals. Free parking. Free drinks. Et cetera, etc.

"'So, how did you do at the craps table?' I ask them. 'No comment,'" says Peter D.

"The truth is that the casinos offer the most free stuff to the biggest losers in the casino. Face it, 'high rollers' is a euphemism. It means loser!" says Peter.

Peter may make some people wince with his bluntness, but his point is not without merit. In order to win comps from a casino you must play big—that is, make big bets and play long, for many hours.

If you are willing to lose enough, and we're talking thousands and thousands, the casino will charter you a jet and fly you to the Super Bowl—their way of putting a big sign on you saying "Biggest Loser."

If you have discovered, as is common, that you actually do better if you play only for a short period of time at each table, then that is the way you should play.

If you feel more comfortable or have better results by betting small at first and maybe gradually increasing as you go along, then that is the way you should play.

If you change your style and bet big right off the bat or bet long hours at a single table, then you are allowing the casino to manage your money for you, and they always manage it the same way: right into their own pocket.

Someone who loses $1,000 at the craps table in order to qualify for a $300 free room, is playing right into the casino's hands. By the same token, a person who loses $100 in order to secure a $25 dinner is a fool.

It is important to remember that the casino is not your friend; it is your seductress.

"Do not let the casino determine how you play craps. Be strong. Do not worry about 'insulting your host.' Stick to your guns. The casino, or any of its employees, are the last place you should look for strategy tips," Peter says.

"Just listen to the dealers sometimes. Although this varies a great deal from casino to casino, the dealers, in their chatter, will never make a truly wise suggestion. They are always—sometimes in a subtle fashion, and sometimes not so subtle—suggesting that you should place a sucker bet, a bet for which the casino's advantage is huge."

CASE HISTORY #13

RAYMOND D.: Anticipating Hot Streaks

The best and easiest way to make a bundle at the craps table is to correctly anticipate the table getting hot. Those who have played craps for any extended period of time know that it is the streakiest game this side of nudist track and field.

Raymond D., a sixty one-year-old lawyer from New York City, has a betting strategy that preys upon streaks and, when he's as hot as the table, devours them for breakfast.

"I always start off playing at the table minimum on the Pass Line," says Ray. "I have to get a feel for how things are flowing. I find that I can read a table by the faces of the players. Obviously, if they look glum I can tell that the table is icy and if everyone is grinning I know the table is hot. Despite this, I always start off at the minimum to gauge how the table is running for me.

"I continue to play the minimum, I'll call that 'one unit.' If I was playing on a five dollar table, then a five dollar chip would be one unit. I play one unit until I am six units up. That way, if the table is running cold, I never bet anything other than the minimum. As you'll see, the hotter the table gets, the higher the bets go, so that I exploit hot streaks to their maximum advantage.

"This is the hardest part of the strategy as far as most players are concerned. They simply lack the patience to pull it off. They are not willing to bet the Come with a minimum bet for the time it might take until the conditions are correct to move on to the next level.

"Impatient players jump the gun and they start placing Odds bets before they have correctly read the table. This is particularly true of a new table in which the other players all seem unusually happy.

"This could mean that the table is hot—or it could mean, just as likely, that the table *was* hot and the other players are slow to figure it out.

"Okay, when I am six units up, I increase each Come bet to two units. If that bet wins, I move up to the next level. If it does not, I return to single unit bets and wait until I am again six units up before I double my bet again.

"To further guard against losing money at a cold table, I walk away if I have lost three consecutive times. I also walk away if, at any time, I am out fifty percent of my stake. I start with a hundred unit stake, as a rule.

"I stay at two units per bet until I am thirteen units up during this time at the table, or until I win three in a row. Then I place a five unit bet on the Pass Line and buy the Odds for the maximum amount. In my case that is Double Odds, so I place five units on the Come and place a ten-unit Odds bet. If those win my next bet is twenty on the Come, forty on the Odds. If those win I raise it again to sixty, one hundred twenty. If at any time I lose, I return to the beginning with one unit bets on the Pass Line.

"The reality of this system is that you spend most of your time at the minimum level, biding your time waiting for the table to get hot, but once it does, things happen fast and furious, and you can make a lot of money in a very short period of time.

"I'm not the only person I know who uses this system, although my levels are uniquely mine. I am more conservative than some others. I know guys who start out with a fifteen dollar minimum bet, even if they are playing on a five dollar table. They jump to five units ($25) after three straight wins and then to a fifteen unit Pass Line bet backed with a thirty unit Odds bet. Their second level is three hundred on the Come, six hundred on Odds, and they peak out at fifteen hundred on the Come, three thousand on the Odds.

"As with an army that can go 'one bridge too far,' some bettors can go one bet too far with a system like this. That is why it is so important that you drop back to a minimum bet after a single loss. You can't afford two losses at that level or you will wipe out all of your winnings.

"One other thing," Ray concludes. "If you are not a mathematician and you enjoy playing Place bets, do not try to translate this strategy into a Place bet strategy—because it won't work. The house advantage for Place bets is much too large for any multi-level betting scheme regarding it to have merit."

CASE HISTORY #14

PETE K.: One-, Two-, and Three-Sail Systems

Pete K. is a thirty-three-year-old newspaper reporter whose job involves a lot of travel. Because of this, he gets to play craps in casinos all over the country. Pete's system, like others we have heard, involves betting in increments depending on previous success.

"I actually have three systems, all of which are related," says Pete. "And the one I choose to play on any given night depends on my mood. I call them the one-sail, two-sail, and three-sail systems.

"If I am feeling extremely conservative, I use the one-sail system. If I feel all right, I use the two-sail system. When I feel as if I have the luck of the world riding with me, I use the three-sail system," he says.

"Here's the one-sail system. Sometimes I call it my button-down-collar system. I start with a ten dollar Pass Line bet, always backing that up with a full Odds bet.

"If the casino allows Double Odds, then I take advantage of that. If they only accept Single Odds, then that is all you will be able to do.

"If I win three times in a row, I increase my Pass Line bet by ten dollars, increasing my Odds bet by ten dollars or twenty dollars, depending on what is allowed.

"If I win three more times in a row, I increase the Pass Line bet by another ten dollars, accompanying that with the maximum Odds bet. If I lose, I return to the beginning of the pattern and start over.

"With the two-sail system, I start out the same way, except I always have one Pass Line and two Come bets. I make my Pass Line bet, taking the full Odds. Then I place a Come bet. When my Come point is determined I back that bet up with full Odds as well. Then I place a second Come bet, and back that up with full Odds when the time comes.

"The three bets are then treated separately, each bet increasing or decreasing by the same increments I described earlier depending on each one's success.

"The three-sail system is the same as the two-sail except that, in addition to the Pass Line bet and two Come bets, I also add on the Six or Eight.

"Assuming Double Odds, if you add that up, you find that I am now betting thirty dollars per round to start on the one-sail system. That increases to sixty dollars after three straight wins.

"With the two-sail system, I play ninety dollars per round once I have all of my bets down. I would suggest that you start with a bankroll of at least six hundred dollars if you are going to play any of these systems—while giving serious thought to walking away if you find that your bankroll is half gone."

CASE HISTORY #15

JACK L.: The 'Don't Ladder' System

Jack L. is a twenty-nine-year-old computer programmer from Bend, Oregon. We'll let Jack tell you his story in his own words.

"I used to use all kinds of extremely complicated craps systems and I wasn't happy with any of them. When I finally found a system that worked for me, I was surprised at how simple it was. I'll cut right to the quick. I don't mind betting on the 'Don't' side. If that is the side that is winning, then that is where I want my chips, and I don't care what the other people at the table think.

"I call my system the 'Don't Ladder.' The system involves betting that a new shooter will not make two straight Pass Line wins.

"Before my first bet I scout out the table and I pick a time when a shooter has made two successful passes and then has Sevened-out.

"Then I start the betting progression with the next shooter. I start with a five-dollar bet on the Don't Pass Line. If I lose, the next bet is a Don't Pass for ten dollars.

"If I win, I stay at five dollars. The basic betting progression is: if I lose, I increase the next bet by five dollars. If I win, I decrease the next bet by five dollars.

"If I lose twice in a row on the same shooter, I stop betting and wait until the next new shooter who qualifies to start the system (that is, he follows a shooter who made at least two consecutive passes before Sevening-out).

"To put it another way, I start with a five-dollar bet against a new shooter. If that bet wins, I make the same bet again. If it loses I place a ten-dollar bet against the shooter's next Come Out roll. If my ten-dollar bet loses I stop betting until there is a new shooter. If the ten-dollar bet is a winner, I go back to five dollars.

"After I get comfortable at the table, I up the ante to the second level of the Don't Ladder System. In the second level I start with a fifteen-dollar bet against the shooter.

"If that bet wins, I place the same bet again. If that bet loses, I place a twenty-dollar bet against the shooter's next Come Out roll. If the twenty-dollar bet wins, I go back to betting fifteen dollars. (If I am feeling particularly daring during that session at the table I go up to thirty dollars instead of twenty dollars if I lose the fifteen-dollar bet.)

"If the twenty-dollar bet loses, I stop and wait for the next qualifying shooter. If I am successful at the second level, I up the ante one more time.

"At the third level I start with a twenty-five dollar bet against the shooter. If that bet wins, I lower the bet to twenty dollars. If the twenty-five dollar bet loses, I bet thirty dollars against the shooter's next Come Out roll. If the thirty-dollar bet wins, I lower the bet to twenty-five dollars. If the thirty-dollar bet loses, I end the session.

"The reason the system works is that every time I break even, that is, lose one and win one, which is what happens most of the time, I make a profit of five dollars. If I am at a table for sixty bets, I win thirty of them and I lose thirty of them, I win one hundred and fifty dollars."

CASE HISTORY #16

CANDACE R.: The Martingale Method I

Candace R. is a fifty-three-year-old restaurateur from Wildwood, New Jersey. She owns a small string of "rest stops" along New Jersey's Highway 9, and is often in Atlantic City on business. When that happens, she always spends her free moments at the craps table.

"I always play at five-dollar minimum/five hundred dollar tables. I find that they are the tables that are most often busy and a busy table is good for my system, since I prefer not to throw the dice myself. Many people think they have to roll the dice when it comes their turn. You just pass them on to the next person and no one will blink," says Candace R.

"I bring with me a bankroll of about seven hundred and fifty dollars. Some players also feel compelled to have at least one bet down for every roll of the dice and that is silly. You should only place bets when the circumstances call for it. Placing a bet on every roll of the dice may help you win some freebies at the casino—and, on the other hand, it may not—but it will not help you win money at the table, and that's the name of the game as far as I am concerned.

"I wait until the shooter has rolled one of the following numbers—Five, Six, Seven, or Eight—three times in a row. What those numbers have in common is that they are all losing rolls if you have a bet on the Field. When it happens, I make a five-dollar bet on the Field."

As we learned earlier, a Field bet wins if a Two, Three, Four, Nine, Ten, Eleven, or Twelve is rolled.

"If I win I take my chips and wait until the next time the Field bet has lost three times in a row, then I place the same bet again. If I lose, that means that four consecutive losing Field numbers have been rolled, so I double the bet to ten dollars.

"If I lose again I move that number up to twenty-five dollars. If I lose again, the number jumps to fifty dollars. Then one hundred dollars. In this manner it always takes only one win to make up all of my losses, plus some.

"In other words, there could be seven straight losing numbers rolled for the Field bet—the three before I started betting and the four times I lost—and then just one winning bet and I am up ten dollars," Candace says.

($5 + $10 + $25 + $50 = $90; $100 − $90 = $10)

It is absolutely essential that you know the maximum bet allowed at your table before you use any system that progresses as dramatically as the Martingale Method.

CASE HISTORY #17

JUDY T.: Place Bet on the Six

Judy T. is a thirty-one-year-old nurse who works at a New Jersey hospital. Here's her story:

"I must be the world's most conservative craps player," Judy says. "I guess that, as far as craps players are concerned, I am a chicken. A scaredy-cat. My system is designed so that I can play for a long time without starting with a tremendous bankroll.

"Perhaps my lack of funds has something to do with my conservative feelings. I get the impression that it isn't going to effect the lifestyle of most players if they lose or not.

"If I lose big at a casino I am going to have to make adjustments in my life to compensate, which puts an additional pressure on me.

"My system starts by making a Place bet on the Six," Judy says. As you recall, this is a bet that a Six will be rolled before the next Seven, and it pays off at a rate of 7-6. Therefore, the Place bet on the Six must be in multiples of six, so that the dealer doesn't have to get out his big scissors and cut chips in half in order to pay off properly.

"When I win my bet, I receive my six dollars back, plus seven dollars more. I place another six dollars, and this time, even if the shooter Sevens-out and I lose, I am still one dollar ahead," she says.

"But, if I win twice in a row, I double my bet, placing twelve dollars on the Six. If I win a third time in a row I go back to the six dollar bet. If I lose, I am two dollars ahead," Judy says.

"And the system continues like that. If you win half the time you make money. If you win more than that, you can do very well, and if you win less than that, you don't lose your shirt. It's the perfect system for the craps player who, for whatever reason, has to count her pennies."

CASE HISTORY #18

BRANDON S.: Inside Numbers

Brandon S. is the fifty-seven-year-old owner of a used-car dealership in a suburb of Philadelphia. He doesn't get to play craps as often as he would like because of his busy schedule, but, ever since the casinos opened in Atlantic City he has tried to make it there four times a year.

During that time, Brandon has devised this, his favorite method of winning at craps:

"My system involves betting the inside numbers—Five, Six, Eight, or Nine," says Brandon. "But I don't start playing until I have waited through at least two shooters, each of whom has rolled at least two inside numbers before Sevening-out. Then, after the Come Out roll of the next shooter, I start to play.

"When I say each, I mean each. I do not mean on the average. If the first shooter throws twenty consecutive inside numbers before Sevening-out and the next shooter only throws one, this still does not qualify as two in a row, each of whom have rolled at least two inside numbers.

"I start by Placing the Six or the Eight for twelve dollars apiece. At the same time, I Place the Five and the Nine for five dollars apiece. I have thirty-four dollars worth of chips down. Remember, I only start after the Come Out roll.

"If the first throw after a point has been determined is a Five or a Nine, I lower my bets on the Six and the Eight to six dollars apiece, and I leave my bets on the Nine and the Five at five dollars each.

"If I win a second time, I take down all of my bets and wait for the correct moment to start over, as per the rules of the system which I have already explained.

("Or, if I see that the table has a history of long runs of inside numbers—remember I observed the patterns of the table before I started playing—I take down my bets on the Five and the Nine and I continue the six dollars bets on the Six and the Eight.")

"If the next roll is a Six or an Eight, I return my bets to the Five and the Nine. If I win four times in a row, I automatically stop and wait for the correct moment to start again.

"If things are not going well, and two shooters in a row have Sevened-out before rolling any inside numbers, I stop playing. I either take a long break before coming back to that table, or I switch tables, once again doing my research on the patterns there before I place my first bet."

CASE HISTORY #19

SKIPPER K.: Long Wait for a Seven (The Martingale Method II)

"To use my method," says Skipper K., a forty-five-year-old vice president for a manufacturing company in Connecticut, "make sure you start out with at least three hundred dollars worth of chips in your tray. Before I start with my theory, let me explain right off the bat that I realize that it lacks mathematical foundation.

"I know that the odds of rolling a Seven remain the same regardless of the history of the dice. But that is also to say that there is no mathematical foundation for a streak, and everyone knows there are streaks in craps.

"Like most craps strategies, the most important aspect of mine is when you start. You must not place a bet until there have been five consecutive rolls of the dice that were NOT Sevens. In other words, I wait until the Seven is good and due.

"Then I place five dollars on the Seven. I know the house advantage is big on this bet, so I have compensated by waiting for a time when—again, contrary to the laws of probability—the Seven is more apt than normal to come up. If I win I take my twenty dollars in profit plus my five-dollar bet and wait until the next time five consecutive non-Sevens were rolled.

"If I lose I bet ten dollars. If I lose again, the bet goes up to twenty dollars. Then forty dollars, then one hundred dollars, then two hundred dollars.

"It is especially important to quit while you are ahead while using this method because eventually thirteen consecutive non-Sevens will be thrown and you will lose a bundle. But the great, great majority of streaks of non-Sevens that make it as far as five rolls do not make it to thirteen, and in each of those cases you turn a profit."

CASE HISTORY #20

BERNARD L.: Don't Pass and Place

Bernard L. is a thirty-seven-year-old reporter for an East Coast trade magazine. His system is far more conservative than the last one we heard:

"The great thing about my system is that it works even when the table is running cold. If you must play on a cold table, switching to this system is an excellent move because it renders you practically disaster-proof. It is almost impossible to lose a lot while using it. I'll explain.

"To put it bluntly, I bet the Don't Pass Line and I keep two place bets going simultaneously. I start out by placing a ten-dollar bet on the Don't Pass. After the shooter has Come Out, I also make two six-dollar Place bets, one apiece in the Six and the Eight. The first time one of my numbers hits I take the money.

"Now I have assured myself of a profit on this round because if a) the shooter Sevens-out at this point, I lose my twelve dollar Place bet but I have already made seven dollars on the one hit and I just made ten dollars more on my Don't Pass bet. So I made five dollars overall.

"When one of my Place bets hit for a second time, I make a Place bet on the Five. The third time it hits I make a Place Bet on the Nine. If the shooter makes his point, I leave all of my Place bets in place. If one of them hits, take the profit off and leave the original bet amount.

"If the shooter throws a Seven or an Eleven on his Come Out roll, then take down all bets and skip that shooter. The worst thing that can happen is that a shooter makes his point right away and then Sevens-out immediately after that. If that happens, I am out twenty-two dollars.

"If the shooter Sevens-out before you hit either of your placed numbers, you lose two dollars. If, as I said before, the shooter throws a Seven after you hit once, you are up five dollars.

"If the shooter makes his point before rolling one of your Placed numbers, you lose ten dollars. If he makes his point after rolling one of your Placed numbers, you only lose three dollars. After two hits, you lose one dollar.

"And, if the shooter hits one of your numbers three times, you are plus one dollar. If I am a loser on three shooters in a row, I take a break or I move to a different table.

"I would suggest that you play this strategy with a bankroll of at least seventy-five dollars, which is much smaller than most systems require."

CHAPTER FOUR
HISTORY OF
DICE GAMES:
THE DIE IS CAST

Every time I roll the dice, and that is daily, I feel as if I am determining fate—as if the fate of the world might hinge in the balance of a single spinning die.

And, as we shall learn in this history of our favorite game, I wasn't the first to feel that way. Dice have been used to make history-changing decisions.

Sophocles claimed that dice were invented in Greece by Palamedes, who taught the game to the soldiers at the siege of Troy three thousand years ago.

But the truth of the matter is that Sophocles did not know and we do not know who invented dice. When mankind began to record history, there were already activities that we would recognize as much like rolling dice.

FATE

Dice were used as a method of solving disputes and determining fate. As far as we can tell, the earliest prehistoric dice were flat two-sided objects.

After that, knucklebones, with four sides, were used. Dem bones seem to have been the direct ancestor of our present-day dotted cubical dice.

Samples of dice-like knucklebones, polished from use, have been found in American prehistoric Indian mounds. One such specimen, unearthed in Florida, was the knucklebone of a fossil llama.

OLDEST TOOL OF GAMBLING

Dice are the oldest tool of gambling known. Evidence of dice games have been found beside the mummies in the tombs of Egypt and ancient Sumeria. In Egypt, dice were rolled by peasants and pharaohs alike. King Rameses III (c. 1182–1151 B.C.) had himself portrayed on the high gate of the temple of Medinet Haboo playing a dice game with two ladies of his harem.

Nice work if you can get it. Ancient Egyptian religious writings mention dice games that are played by the spirits of the departed in the underworld.

GREEK AND ROME

Dice were an accepted form of gambling during both the Greek and the Roman Empires. Augustus and Nero rolled 'em. Caligula, predictably enough, was a notorious dice cheat.

The Roman emperors used dice that were cast from conical beakers of carved ivory and the dice were sometimes of crystal inlaid with gold. Most dice, however, were made out of bones, although dice made of ivory were not unknown. Other materials that were used include porcelain, amber, marble, alabaster, and bronze.

Dice found in a Roman tomb from the first century B.C. were even the same as those used today in that the sum of the spots on opposite sides is always Seven.

According to one Roman historian: "Loaded dice were not uncommon and one mis-spotted die bearing two fours suggests that cheating was known and practiced by Roman mechanics. In addition to the anklebone, the Greeks and Romans also used the tesserae or cubical six-sided dice, both sometimes being employed in the same game."

These were thrown from dicing cups containing crossbars to prevent the cheater from sliding the die in a predetermined position.

Yes, dice games date back more than two thousand years. We use the word games advisedly as some of the dice games of antiquity were matters of life and death. When Julius Caesar decided to ignore the edict of Rome and take his victorious army across the Rubicon, he spoke like a true craps player.

"Lacta alea est," he said.

The die is cast.

EUROPE

And that wasn't the only time that dice have been used to decide matters which would have an effect on world history. According to the legend, in 1020 A.D. the king of Norway and the king of Sweden, both named Olaf, met at Konungahella in Norway to decide who would get the district of Hising. They decided to roll the dice. Highest roll won the land. According to the legend, the Swedish king threw two Sixes. The King of Norway took his turn and also rolled Boxcars. The Swedish king re-threw, and again had two Sixes. On the Norwegian king's second throw, one die showed a Six but the other split in two, so there were seven dots showing. Norway gained the district and it is reported that the kings parted at the end of the meeting great friends.

Dice-playing increased greatly in popularity in England during the twelfth and thirteenth centuries A.D. The favorite game was called Hazard and men gambled when playing it.

A man could win the slave labor of his competitor with a roll of the dice until that was made illegal. After that, the worst a man could blow on one roll of the dice was his life savings, and the clothes off his back.

In 1190, it was illegal for the lower-ranked Crusaders under England's Richard I and Philip of France from playing at any sort of game for money.

Knights and clergymen could play Hazard for money but were penalized one hundred shillings if caught losing more than twenty shillings in a twenty-four-hour period.

Elmer de Multone was indicted in 1311 "for being a common night walker; and, in the day, is wont to entice strangers and persons unknown, to a tavern, and there deceive them by using false dice."

CRABS

However, in the somewhat grimier London of Charles Dickens, the game was known as "Crabs," which was the English term for a pair of ones.

When the French picked up the game they pronounced the name with a fine *français* fervor: "Craps!" That game was a tad more complex than the one we play today.

AFRICA

In Africa, as with the rest of the world, dice are today used predominantly for gambling—although the games that are played are sometimes based on old fortune-telling beliefs.

NORTH AMERICA

American Indians, back in the days before the settlers showed up and ruined everything, used to make their dice out of fruit pits, animal bone, or shells.

They would put many of these objects in a basket. The basket would then be raised—very dramatically, of course—and then "brought smartly to the ground."

The sides of the objects which showed would determine "the count." The Cheyenne Indians marked the sides of their dice—which they made out of plum pits—to better differentiate them, just as the six sides of a die are marked so that no two sides are the same.

But the Cheyenne did not use dots. They used blanks, crosses, and a symbol that was supposed to represent the foot of a bear. They would roll five plum pits at a time. Two bears and three crosses won the jackpot.

An Indian tribe, hailing from what is today the State of Washington, known as the Twanas, used beaver teeth as their dice. The tooth either landed up or down.

One of the dice had a string tied around its middle, and this was the one that counted the most. The highest score possible came when the stringed die landed up and the others all landed down. There were legends of dice cheats who knew just how to hold the beaver teeth in hand to get the desired roll.

THE OCCULT

Gambling and settling disputes are two of the things that rolling dice have been used for, but there is another category of dice rolling that we have not yet touched upon: The occult. Rolling dice has been used over the years to do some pretty spooky stuff.

The Abantu tribes in Africa used to roll the dice once a month. On the night of the new moon, the village witch doctor would roll dice in front of each home to determine the fortunes of the occupants for the month. Dr. Livingstone (we presume) used to call these men "dice doctors." The dice doctor doubled as a private eye as he also used the dice to determine the identity of thieves.

CRAPS IN THE U.S.

Craps was brought to America by settlers and it was in the New World that the rules we associate as those of craps were cemented down.

Craps games in the United States were played on blankets in alleys, riverboats, and wharves up and down the East Coast of the United States.

As the frontiersmen moved west, they took craps with them. One day the game reached Nevada—and God looked down and saw that this was a Good Thing.

Today, it has been estimated that as many as thirty million Americans play craps every year.

CHAPTER FIVE
TOURNAMENT
STRATEGY

Some casinos offer craps tournaments, usually held weekly. Some are free to enter while some cost as much as one thousand dollars to enter. When the entry fee is that high, however, you usually get a complimentary room in the hotel for the weekend, free meals, and maybe a free cocktail or two.

And, it should be noted, the craps tournaments with the highest entrance fees usually have the highest prizes as well. Sometimes these tourneys have first prizes as large as fifty thousand dollars. It is the ratio of entrance fee to prize money that tells you how stingy or generous a tournament is. In most tournaments the top ten finishers receive a prize of some sort.

Strategy changes when you play in a tournament, since you have stopped playing against the house and instead are playing against the other players in the tournament.

Instead of playing over-the-long-run strategy, you will have to make as much money as you can within some constraint, usually a time limit (an hour) or a certain number of rolls (say one hundred).

If the tournament is large enough, it will be held in rounds. After an hour, say, the top three players move on to the next round and everybody else is through.

It isn't even necessary to win money to win a craps tournament. If everyone loses, then the player who loses the least wins the grand prizes.

So, for obvious reasons, players who compete regularly in craps tournaments have learned to keep an eye on everyone else's chips as well as their own.

KNOW THE RULES

If you decide to enter several tournaments in different casinos, make sure that you are familiar with the rules of each tournament. Rules differ from tourney to tourney and you could lose money playing one tournament by the rules of another. (Some tournaments even change the rules from round to round. Stay alert.)

One common rule difference has to do with whether or not you must place a Pass or Don't Pass bet on every play—although you are always allowed to make other bets as well. Some tournaments forbid Proposition bets of greater than twenty-five dollars. Some tournaments allow you to keep your chips covered, others require that they remain visible.

Some tournaments allow you to purchase chips with your own money if you lose all of your tournament chips, while others say you lose when your tournament chips are gone.

Don't worry about rule differences too much, however, as there is almost always an orientation meeting before the tournament starts to make sure that everyone knows what rules they are playing by. Just make sure you are paying attention.

TOURNEY-SPECIFIC SYSTEMS

There are bets in craps tournaments that you would rarely see on a regular casino table. For example, imagine that time is running out in a tournament round and you are in last place. There are only a few rolls of the dice to go. It might behoove you to put your remaining chips on the Two or the Twelve, the longest shots on the board. Normally, this would be considered a foolish bet, but under these circumstances it is absolutely the correct thing to do.

If you are in second place, then you definitely have to keep an eye on the player in first place. If he starts copying your bets—knowing that if you both win or lose the same amount until the end of the time period, he will still be in first place and you will still be in second—you are going to have to change your style.

If you are the player in second place, matching the bets of the player in the lead is no way to catch up.

TYPE OF TOURNEY PLAYERS

Tournament players come in two sorts: Some will play very conservatively, using (most likely) the same strategy they use when they are playing against the house.

Others go wild. They play Hardways and Proposition bets. Experience tells us that, even within the time constraints of the craps tournament, overly aggressive players still run out of chips very rapidly.

SEPARATE YOURSELF FROM THE PACK

It is, likewise, difficult for players who are too conservative to win tournaments since there is usually more than one such player in each tournament and they form a pack of players whose luck is running the same.

It is often necessary to be selectively aggressive in such circumstances in order to break out of the conservative pack.

Here's a suggestion from one expert: "Let's say the leader has one hundred dollars on the Pass Line and the point is Four. He takes two hundred dollar Odds. You could then lay the Four for two hundred dollars. If a Seven rolls, you've suddenly managed to put yourself four hundred dollars ahead, as he would have lost three hundred dollars and you won one hundred dollars."

Being creative is key. One of the most exciting things about craps tournaments is the way things can change on the last few rolls of the dice.

And, for those whose social lives are wrapped up in the casino rhythm, playing in craps tournaments is an excellent way to make like-minded friends.

CHAPTER SIX
RULES OF THUMB &
SUPERSTITIONS

RULES OF THUMB

1. It is never a good idea to lose your entire bankroll in any one night of shooting dice. It is psychologically damaging to "come home broke." Therefore, I recommend that you make a pledge to yourself before you start that you will walk away if your bankroll diminishes to 20 percent of its original size. Chances are, once you fall that far behind you are not going to return to the break-even point, not on that night anyway. Cut your losses.

2. Find out the minimum bet allowed at a table before you start playing. Do not play over your head. Determine your "comfort level." If you play at a rate beyond that, you are asking for trouble.

3. Find out the maximum bet allowed at a table before you start playing at it. Many potentially winning craps strategies compensate for slow losses with quick winnings, and you do not want to discover that the betting maximum prohibits you from making a bet just as you are about to make a killing (or get back your losses).

4. One last note regarding minimum and maximum bets at a table: If you played on a table on Saturday night and its minimum and maximum bets were within your personal specifications, and now you are playing on that same table on a Wednesday morning, do not assume that the minimum and maximum bets are the same as they were. Many casinos change those numbers depending on both the day of the week and the time of day.

5. Never play craps when you are feeling desperate, either financially or emotionally. If you are even considering an "all or nothing" bet at a craps table, you are not in the correct frame of mind to be there and you should walk away immediately.

6. When placing an Odds bet, find out the maximum amount allowed (always some factor of the mandatory Come or Pass Line bet that must first be placed). The maximum amount allowed will always be the bet with the fairest payoff. The larger (one-times, two-times, three-times, etc.) the Odds bet allowed, the lower the house advantage on that bet, although the advantage never quite reduces itself to zero because of the house advantage in the mandatory Come or Pass Line bet.

7. If you are playing craps outside the United States, find out if tipping is legal before you attempt to give

your dealer a token of your appreciation. Casinos in New Zealand, Australia, and England forbid tipping, as do most casinos in Europe and Asia.

8. If a dealer notices that you are playing a system that is working and attempts to engage you in conversation about it, clam up. Play dumb. Even if the query comes from a fellow player, resist the urge to explain. Be vague. Claim that you are making up your bets as you go along. (It is okay to discuss your system with a fellow player away from the table, but never at the table.)

9. If you find your dealer rude, or if for some other reason you are not getting along with your dealer, move. Even if you are annoyed with a fellow player at the table, get up and play somewhere else. Do not stick around. If you stay your aggravation and stress will only worsen and nobody wins if a fight breaks out.

10. It is okay to have a couple of drinks when you are playing craps but do not drink to excess. It is much more difficult to to remain disciplined and stick with a strategy if you have had too much to drink. However, most players at any given table will be drinking, so it is a good idea to sip at a drink now and again as it will make it easier for you to blend in with the craps "amateurs."

CRAPS SUPERSTITIONS

There are a number of craps superstitions that you need to know about. It isn't because these superstitions have any scientific or mathematical credibility—if they did, they wouldn't be superstitions, would they?—it is that you need to know about them so that you won't inadvertantly make enemies at the craps table.

1. If the rolled dice touch someone's hand, that roll will be a Seven. So if you hear someone shouting: "Watch your hands!" as the shooter starts to roll, take heed. Even the casino crew will shout this out and be careful of where they place their hands. Folks have been known to accuse the casino of jinxing the roll by allowing the dice to hit a dealer's hand.

2. Never throw money on the table to cash in while the shooter is shooting when a good roll is in progress. If the dice hit the new money, the next roll will be a Seven.

3. When the dice or a die leaves the table, the next roll will be a Seven. This might be avoided by making sure that the dealers give you the same dice for your next roll. This is why you'll hear the shooter yell out: "Same dice!"

4. Then there is the Virgin Principle: A woman who has never rolled the dice will have a hot roll the first time out. Female dice virgins are a much sought-after breed. When one appears, the veteran players will sometimes place bets for her to better take advantage of her virginal powers.

5. Men who have never rolled the dice before will have bad rolls—losers that they are.

6. Never be the first or only player at a table. Dice are chilly at a new table and need to be bounced around a

bit—by someone else, of course—before they start to glow.

7. As we've discussed, wrong bettors are not very popular. Not only are they usually betting against everyone else at the table, they are thought to have mystical powers over the dice. A wrong bettor at a table will increase the likelihood of the Seven coming up. And the more wrong bettors at a table, the more the Seven will come up.

GLOSSARY

ACE The one spot on a die.

"An ace."

ACTION Amount of money wagered by a gambler in a casino. Casinos base their perks on the amount of action a player is giving them.

ANY CRAPS This is a type of bet placed on one roll of the dice, and it does not matter which roll it is. You bet that a Two, Three, or Twelve will come up on the next roll. If it does, you win—at a payoff of 7–1. If any other number is rolled, you lose.

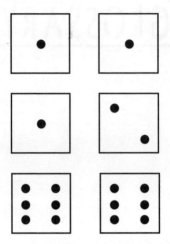

"ANY CRAPS is a winning bet if one of these combinations comes up on the next roll of the dice."

BACK LINE See DON'T PASS LINE.

BANKROLL The amount of money you brought with you for gambling.

BET RIGHT Betting with the shooter.

BET THE DICE TO LOSE You bet that the shooter will not make his or her point; betting against the shooter.

BET THE DICE TO WIN You bet the shooter will make his or her point; betting with the shooter.

BET WRONG Betting against the shooter.

BIG EIGHT You bet that an Eight will be rolled before a Seven. This bet pays even money.

BIG SIX You bet that a Six will be rolled before a Seven. This bet pays even money.

BOXCARS Roll a Twelve; two Sixes.

BOXMAN The casino employee who sits at the center of the table and is in charge of the table.

CHANGE COLOR Exchanging your chips for those of a different denomination.

CHECKS Chips.

COME BET This bet is placed only after the roller rolls a Come point. After that, it behaves just like a Pass Line bet.

COME OUT ROLL A shooter's first roll. The roll to shoot a natural or establish a point.

CRAPS When a Two, Three, or Twelve is thrown.

CREW The dealers and stickman. The boxman is not considered a part of the table's crew.

DEUCE The two spot on a die.

DON'T COME BET This bet is placed only after the roller rolls a Come point. The bet then behaves just like a Don't Pass bet.

DON'T PASS BET You bet that the player who is rolling the dice will either roll a Two or a Three on the first roll, or that, after rolling a Come point, that the roller will roll a Seven before matching the point. If a Twelve is rolled on the first roll, it is a push and no money exchanges hands. If a natural is rolled, you lose. A Don't Pass bet, of course, must be placed before the shooter rolls the dice to establish a point.

DOUBLE ODDS An Odds bet that is twice as large as the Pass Line or Come bet that preceded it.

EASY WAY Rolling a Four, Six, Eight, or Ten other than by rolling a pair.

EVEN MONEY A 1–1 payoff. Bet a chip to win a chip.

FIELD BETS You bet that a Two, Three, Four, Nine, Ten, Eleven, or Twelve is rolled before a Five, Six, Seven, or Eight. Twos and Twelves pay double.

FLOORMAN Supervisor of several tables.

FREE ODDS Bets made only in conjunction with Come or Don't Come bets which pay off according to the genuine probability of that result.

FRONT LINE Another term for Pass Line.

GEORGE Dealer lingo for a good tipper.

HARDWAY Rolling a Four, Six, Eight, or Ten by rolling a pair.

HARDWAY BETS In this bet, you are wagering on the results of each die rather than on the sum total of the dice. If you bet Three/Three, you win if both dice come up Three. A Two and a Four is still a Six but does not win. The Hardway numbers must come up before a Seven is rolled for the Hardway bet to be a winner.

HOPPING A bet on one roll of the dice. The house advantage is huge on hop bets, so they should be avoided. Bets that should pay 35–1 will only pay 29–1 and bets that should pay 17–1 only pay 15–1.

HOT ROLL Series of rolls in which numbers other than the Seven come up.

INSIDE NUMBERS Five, Six, Eight, or Nine.

LAYOUT The design on a craps table that shows the players where to place their chips in order to place particular types of bets.

MECHANIC A cheater.

NATURAL A Seven or Eleven thrown on the Come Out roll.

"OFF" Verbal instruction to the dealer that a particular bet has been withdrawn for that roll of the dice.

ON THE HOP A bet on one roll of the dice.

ONE ROLL BET Any bet that is in action for a single roll of the dice, i.e., Any Craps, Field, Any Seven. Also known as Hopping or being on the Hop.

PASS A natural on the first roll or shooter makes an established point.

PASS LINE You bet that the player who is rolling the dice will either roll a Seven or Eleven on the first roll, or match his point, if there is one. A Two, Three, or Twelve on the first roll loses for a Pass Line bet, as does a player who rolls a Seven before matching his point. This type of bet, of course, must be placed before the Come Out roll. This is, by far, the most popular bet at the table. It is the fact that, at any given time, most craps players have chips on the Pass Line, that brings about such a camaraderie at the craps table, with (almost) everyone rooting for the shooter to make his passes.

PIT A group of craps tables clustered together in a casino.

PLACE BETS After the shooter has rolled a point, you pick a number and bet that it comes up before the shooter rolls a Seven. Since different numbers come up with different frequencies, all Place bets do not payoff at the same rate.

Fours and Tens pay off 9–5. Fives and Nines pay off at 7–5. Eights and Sixes pay off at 7–6. Place bets on Six and Eight are the most common bets.

POINT Any Four, Five, Six, Eight, Nine, or Ten a player throws on the Come Out roll. This number becomes the shooter's point and must be rolled again before the shooter rolls a Seven.

PROPOSITION BETS These are made on a shooter's first roll of the dice only. You may make a Proposition bet on Two, Three, Eleven, or Twelve. Two and Twelve pay off at 30–1, whereas Three and Eleven pay off at 15–1.

PUSH Term used in all forms of gambling, meaning a tie.

SEVEN-OUT The shooter has rolled a Seven before his or her point, and now must pass the dice to the next shooter.

SHOOTER The player who rolls the dice.

SINGLE ODDS An Odds bet that equals the Pass Line or Come bet it accompanies. When Odds betting was first allowed, Single Odds were the maximum bet you could make. But, because of competition between the casinos, Double and Triple Odds bets are now allowed in some places, further reducing the house advantage.

SLIDER A cheater who, when rolling the dice, slides them rather than rolls them so that the side on top stays the same.

SNAKE EYES Roll a two; two aces.

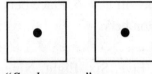

"Snake eyes."

STAKE The amount of money you come to the table with.

STICKMAN Craps dealer who expertly maneuvers the dice back to the shooter with his big stick.

VIG House advantage.

WALK The amount of money you walk away from the table with. To find your net win for the session, you subtract your stake from your walk. To discover your net loss, you subtract your walk from your stake.

WIN LINE Another term for Pass Line.

"WORKING" Verbal instruction given by the stickman indicating that all bets are currently in effect for the next roll of the dice.

WRONG BETTORS Those who place Don't Pass Line and Don't Come bets.

YO Eleven. As in "throw a yo to the dealer," in the form of a tip.

"A Yo."

BIBLIOGRAPHY

Andersen, Ian. *Turning the Tables on Las Vegas.* New York: The Vanguard Press, 1976.

Ford, Roger L. *Advantage Craps.* Albuquerque, New Mexico: Silverthorne Publications, 2000.

Gallagher, Thomas B. *Craps Made Simple.* Santa Barbara, California: The Thomas Company, 1993.

Gollehon, John. *Conquering Casino Craps.* Grand Rapids, Michigan: Gollehon Books, 1997.

Roto, Robert R. *Casino Craps.* New York: Barricade Books, 1999.

Scoblete, Frank. *Beat the Craps out of the Casinos.* Chicago, Illinois: Bonus Books, Inc., 1991.

———. *Forever Craps.* Chicago, Illinois: Bonus Books, Inc., 2000.